Private Sector by Head
Public Sector by Heart

Private Sector by Head
Public Sector by Heart

Full of guidance and observations from experienced commercial and procurement professionals

BROWN DOG BOOKS

First published 2022

Published under licence by Brown Dog Books and
The Self-Publishing Partnership Ltd, 10b Greenway Farm, Bath Rd,
Wick, nr. Bath BS30 5RL

www.selfpublishingpartnership.co.uk

ISBN paperback: 978-1-83952-392-2
ISBN hardback: 978-1-83952-393-9
ISBN e-book: 978-1-83952-394-6

Cover design by Kevin Rylands incorporating artwork from Spencer Hill,
based on an idea by Suzy Valentine
Internal design by Mac Style
Cartoons by Spencer Hill

Printed and bound in the UK
This book is printed on FSC certified paper

MIX
Paper from responsible sources
FSC® C013604

Contents

Foreword

For those who care about supply chain, this book is a godsend. It is not about systems, process, structures and reporting lines. If you want such advice, try an internet search for the answers. This book is different. It is different because it is about real life and written by practitioners, probably people much like you.

I spent over 30 years in supply chain with airlines, a technology start-up and an oil and gas major. Each company I worked for knew the success associated with great supply chain management. Dramatic, unexpected failure was, however, never far away. Money was lost in huge sums, and reputations tarnished forever when things went wrong. Today, and working as a university lecturer, I have no doubt that at least as much can be learned from error as it can from success. The challenge is getting people to talk about it and share their reflections. High praise to 4C for managing to build the relationship of trust, so necessary with the right people for this book to emerge.

There is no fundamental reason that practice in private and public sectors should differ. Situations vary but, surely, the similarities outweigh the differences. I believe the material issue is something to do with confidence and belief. You will see that here: that behaviours and leadership, at all levels, stand out as the characteristics that shape outcomes. PowerPoint might tell a story but it cannot make decisions, generate fun, passion or purpose. I am glad it cannot do so, because that is *your* job. No system, machine or artificial intelligence is going to do these things for you. This is both your challenge and your privilege. Your success is down to you and those around you.

This book draws from the experiences of those who make decisions, under intense pressure, in sometimes desperate circumstances. If you have read this far, you probably agree that a book about supply chain, that tells the truth, talks openly about both success and failure, is long overdue. Make the most of it. It might just reshape your future.

My plea to you is that you turn away from your laptop, walk away from your desk and turn to the Introduction. I promise you it will be well worth your time to do so. Be curious and travel hopefully.

Paul Alexander
Teaching Fellow
University of Portsmouth

Biography

Paul Alexander has spent over 30 years working in procurement and supply chain. After leaving university in 1986, he started professional life with Trans Australia Airlines as a Purchasing Officer and after two years, moved to British Airways (BA) as an Engineering Buyer. BA was a great environment to grow a career at this time and saw Paul move from engineering into crew union negotiations and overseas contracting activities across the globe.

The rise of the dot-com boom took him to work in the United States, where he worked on fast-evolving supply chain technology solutions with Cordiem. After that, he saw an impressive start-up company sadly destined to fail after the shock of 9/11. The experience of managing a company, as it faced closure, was a pivotal professional experience, and one that shaped Paul's attitudes to business life forever.

Paul returned across the Atlantic to BA where, after a spell leading supplier relationship management, he led BA's £4 billion fleet renewal programme for procurement. Thereafter, he became Head of Procurement and led the function as it weathered the rise of low-cost competition and several oil price shocks that threatened the airline's very existence.

The opportunity to join BP was compelling and Paul moved – both sector and company – in 2009, to act as Head of Region for BP Procurement (BP). Services and fossil fuels were new challenges and the experience good, with BP looking for a complete overhaul in the way it achieved value in its management of supply markets.

Paul moved into higher education at the University of Portsmouth in 2019. It is now time to reflect, to write, to learn and inspire a new generation of supply chain practitioners.

Paul is married to Claire, has two sons, Adam and Joseph, is a rower, cyclist, poor guitarist and model railway nut. He is a Fellow of CIPS and has an MBA from Lancaster University.

Introduction

'Quality is never an accident; it is always the result of high intention, sincere effort, intelligent direction and skillful execution; it represents the wise choice of many alternatives.'

William A Foster, United States Marine (1915–1945)

Background

This book is not a 'textbook' about procurement processes, nor is it meant to be consumed like a novel… Instead it is an engaging handrail, full of guidance and observations from experienced commercial professionals with a passion to share their learning.

Let me attempt to set the scene.

Public sector organisations are, by their very nature, not driven by the need to make profit but by the need to benefit the communities they serve. They operate, in general, with money sourced from taxes, donations and gifts. Any surplus is normally reinvested and not returned to investors as dividends.

Across the public sector, profitability can best be expressed as operational capability. But to state that the public sector departments and agencies are not businesses is a misnomer – they are, indeed, very much businesses, just not remunerated at the point of use nor in a single transaction. But they do, indeed, transact cash for goods, works and services, much the same as the private sector.

Why this book?

So why this publication? Well, principally for two reasons:

1. Firstly, to dispel the myth that private sector is good and public sector is bad…

And to:

2. Provoke thought and dialogue, in order to highlight the need to raise commercial acumen in the public sector.

This 'handrail' to achieving good commercial practice in the public sector is nothing more than that – a steadying assistance to help marshal numerous confusing volatile challenges. Whilst these sometimes seem like an insurmountable tsunami, they can be overcome when broken down to basics, ordered, analysed and faced with the collaboration of others. We felt the need to share our thoughts because none of us has come across a single publication that addresses all the issues that we encounter on a daily basis. Our aim is to shed a light on those matters and not provide specific solutions.

With no slight intended towards our colleagues in the world of accountancy, two plus two has always been four, and always will be, whereas the way I spend the 'four' will depend upon volatile market forces and is dynamic by its very nature. That is why commercial activity and procurement are both exciting and the only elements that executives have any real power to change. It is the way they do business, and not to exercise that power when necessary is folly. We, therefore, seek change, endorsed by the highest leadership and exercised throughout the organisation to build commercial acumen and continuously improve outcomes for our end-customers.

In an environment where change is constant, not only with regulation and constraints but also where different outputs will need a range of different inputs, there is little point in trying to provide single cover-all solutions. Because markets are constantly shifting, this publication introduces topics that are ever-present in a changing environment and points to the latest evolving thinking on them. Throughout the book, we recommend continuous engagement and research to keep up-to-date with the detail of developments and evolved practices. Peers, colleagues and the internet are key to this. This book does not attempt to reiterate the actual process of procurement – managing tenders, running competitions and letting, ending or renegotiating contracts. There are many longer reference texts that can do that.

Procurement is not just about buying. It is a fundamental part of the commercial operation of any organisation. There is a perception that someone with financial acumen in the public sector can evaluate the impact of a business decision through financial statements and wellbeing in the long term. More worryingly, some believe that this is, of itself, good enough. Put simply, if £19.5m is spent from a budget of £20m leaving £0.5m in reserve, while mathematically correct, the calculation fails absolutely to define a good commercial position, without balanced reasoning on what value and outcomes are created.

Properly developed commercial acumen goes far beyond mere numbers and balance sheets. It seeks to ensure outcomes that deliver the most benefit to all aspects of the business. It evaluates and balances the impact and relationship with many other factors including people, processes, and strategic aims, instead of just knowing that 97.5 per cent of the budget has been spent in a legally and regulatorily compliant way. Commercial acumen will enable an understanding of where £19.5m was spent, on what, with whom and why and, most importantly, what benefit was derived from it.

It's worth noting here that the terms 'acumen' and 'success' are subjective and not always about making or saving the most money. Top-level success for one organisation may be measured in vastly different ways to another.

Who is the book for?

If you rely on the provision of any goods, works or services either to complete your role or provide a service to your customers, this is the book for you. Whilst some chapters focus on topics that will be most relevant to procurement professionals, most chapters examine a topic from multiple viewpoints, encouraging readers to consider procurement from the view of Chief Executive, internal customer, contract manager and the ultimate contract beneficiary. The optimal results will only be achieved by all parts of an organisation working together, and to do this, all stakeholders must understand the importance of their contribution, and how commercial decision-making is at the heart of delivering organisational strategies.

The regulatory environment

The Public Contracts Regulations 2015 (PCRs) are both stringent and rigorous for good reason to ensure propriety and protect the public purse, but they are often interpreted and followed to the detriment of the desired outcomes. This is unsurprising given the high value and level of complexity that often accompany many public projects; however, public sector procurement can range from the mundane to the incredibly complicated. With such a broad contracting landscape, the countless rules and legislation governing the various processes can be an all-consuming minefield. This is especially so for those who simply process everything within the boundaries that are governed by these constraints. As a consequence, there are considerable challenges facing those who manage public procurement projects at a strategic level and seek unshackled innovation in areas unconstrained by legacy controls.

It is a cheap shot to label the public sector as an uninspiring and unimaginative monolith, but perhaps there is an element of truth in some of the criticism, which can be summarised by the following passage from Mariana Mazzucato, Professor of Economics at University College London, who states, '*...if value is created collectively, then those who pursue a career in the public sector should also be taught how to think outside the box, and how to be entrepreneurial. But* *they aren't'.*[1] Perhaps a little unfair at first sight but stated by someone with unparalleled experience in the matter.

The lack of commercial strategic thinking is blamed on two key issues which the public sector faces:

1. The PCRs obstruct commercial skills being brought to bear.
2. The budgetary constraints placed on the public sector discourage commercial acumen being applied.

These statements, whilst having a familiar ring to them, are of course untrue.

It is fair to say that the imposition of what was EU legislation bound in the PCRs has created an environment of concentration on rigid adherence to regulatory provision and, therefore, an understanding shift towards 'output' rather than 'outcome-based solutions'. The regulations can be cumbersome and require wise interpretation to navigate successfully and ensure that value for money is achieved. They can appear to impair rather than ensure value for money, but only if they are wrongly applied. This book explores how the best outcomes can be achieved within the regulatory environment and transparently deliver value for money for end-users.

The perception that commercial acumen is repressed among procurement professionals by budgetary constraints is also unfounded. The restraints may present additional challenges, but this book will also outline how good research, preparation and collaboration across the enterprise can not only allow – but positively encourage – entrepreneurial spirit to flourish.

Focus your efforts on the biggest value-adding areas

Any organisation, private or public, that relies upon suppliers to deliver goods, works and services to carry out their mission must:

1. Treat the suppliers with respect.
2. Involve suppliers and others who use their services in designing 'how' the relevant services are best delivered to ensure value for money for the buyer and a profitable outcome for the supplier. Both are of equal importance to a sustainable outcome.
3. Avoid process over substance.
4. Focus on outcomes and not outputs. Tell the market what you want to do, not how to do it – outputs are normally easy to measure and relatively easy to achieve but rarely deliver the required outcomes. Outcomes should drive outputs – never the other way round.

---

1. Mazzucato, M. (2011) *The Entrepreneurial State: Debunking Public vs Private Sector Myths.*

OUTCOMES – defines what the business or its customers wants or needs to achieve.
OUTPUTS – are the actions, activities or process that contribute to achieving an outcome.

5. The vast majority of time should be spent on the specification and pre-market work, with the very close second priority on the contract management regime designed with the supplier (not imposed upon them), with the smallest concentration of effort on the process; process is well-documented elsewhere and is not the focus of this book.
6. Don't fall into the trap of thinking anyone 'can do procurement' – you would not have a non-qualified accountant as a CFO, nor would you employ a vet as a doctor – so ensure that your Head of Procurement, or even better your Commercial Director, is appropriately qualified and is at the right level in the organisation.

For too long, emphasis and time has been expended on the 'process' of procurement and insufficient on the 'planning' and 'contract management' elements where the largest commercial impact can be gained.

What is required is a flattening, if not inverting, of the effort curve as illustrated in the figure below:

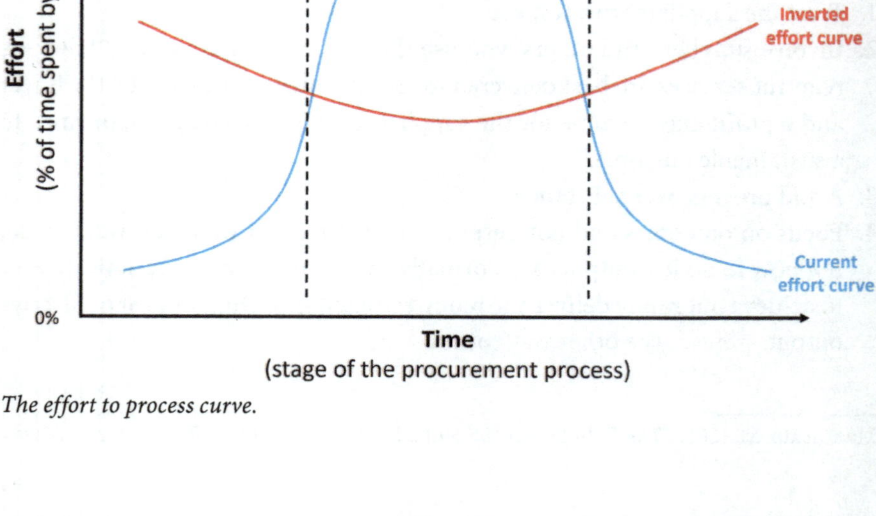

The effort to process curve.

The complexity and legal requirements of procurement regulations can lead to detailed procurement management demanding an enormous investment from the public authority.

Unfortunately, this leaves little additional space or energy for those vital qualitative considerations which have the potential to make the crucial difference between 'good' procurement and just 'well-regulated' procurement. These challenges are exacerbated by the fact that the PCRs change every second year. Those involved in procurement (not just the professional procurement staff), therefore, need to be aware of the challenges and, more importantly, the benefits that any new legislation will bring so that they can be managed and exploited.

Timelines are next to godliness

Lack of time to undertake adequate preparation is the first enemy of effective procurement. Procurement can be improved immeasurably by making time at the pre-planning stage to take a radical and critical view of the current or traditional arrangements, ensuring that one comprehends the true cost of procurement, and genuinely understanding the market with which one is engaging.

Current doctrine demands that those undertaking public procurement must adopt a more commercial approach. It doesn't necessarily say how. One key factor is appreciating that the true cost of a contractually binding procurement agreement does not lie in the price alone. It is vital for the procurement specialist to understand from the outset what the *total* cost of ownership of a service or item will be over the lifetime of the contract and in its immediate aftermath. These costs incorporate not only the initial purchase, but those associated with installing, operating, maintaining, updating and, ultimately, even disposing of assets or services which may be highly complex or technical. An exemplar of this is when a housing association concentrates on minimising the cost of the construction of new housing stock by specifying gas boilers with an anticipated lifespan of only six years when the maintenance budget is based on a lifespan of 10 years… The 'kicking the financial can down the road' syndrome.

The best leaders take procurement and their whole supply chain seriously. To quote Jeff Bezos, when discussing supply chain: *'If you don't understand the details of your business you will fail'.*

If the private sector fails, it fails its shareholders. Due to this, the private sector has absolute imperatives which are to continue to exist and to make money – to do so it either builds its product or service for less, makes it last longer (which enables you to sell it for greater return) or sells more of them, and preferably all three! Avoiding failure in the public sector is more important, because if it does not, it fails the public it is there to serve, and it should recognise the commercial imperatives of the private sector, emulating them where applicable. This passion to deliver for the public good with the same commercial imperative of the private sector is what drives all the book's authors and led to our naming this book 'Private Sector by Head, Public Sector by Heart'.

Industry has learnt that selling more is not always within its gift; however, building for less and making it last longer both are. Pivotal to achieving these two goals is managing the supply chain. This is still complex because supply chains are not static and managing them is a persistent activity.

This author, when visiting a FTSE 100 company, noted that in the CEO's office was a large display screen on one of the four walls showing the firm's top 20 suppliers, a headline of what was supplied, how much was spent with them and the start and end of the contract. This was updated daily. He expected managers at every level to know their own contract spend, and 20 per cent of their remunerations were based on the successful leverage of their element of the supply chain.

His CFO realised the power of the supply chain and it was more closely managed than any other element – the company's view was it had more influence on that proportion of spend versus the other key cost drivers (staff and real estate), neither of which it could truly affect without increasing supply chain spend in the process.

Whilst public sector profitability does not exist *per se*, we must view it as being operational efficacy. That is, getting more or better (or both) for the same or less. The public sector's supply chain is integral to and essential for the very goods, works and services to deliver their outputs and outcomes, but how many in the sector can honestly say they know it inside out?

Accordingly, not only do we need to ensure that continuous improvement across the length of any commercial agreement is included but is properly managed to ensure that what has been promised is, indeed, being delivered. To manage contracts effectively is a skill and it is imperative that the staff responsible for it are properly trained, empowered and up to date with current legislation, regulation and market developments.

The National Audit Office frequently and regularly criticises the whole of the public sector in its reports to Parliament, but the main targets for much of this criticism are central government departments. With some notable exceptions, central government shapes legislation, sets regulation, funds, and directs delivery across the public sector. However, it is at a local level in local authorities, housing associations, hospital trusts, higher education, further education, utilities and schools that the money is spent on delivery to the front line. This is where the development and maintenance of commercial acumen will ensure the greatest benefit.

Why listen to me?

I am evangelical about procurement and the wider commercial function of which it is a part. I am so because I have seen the benefit of wise commercial delivery at a local level, at one end of the spectrum, and at the other, seen soldiers lose their lives and families lose their loved ones when it has been applied badly or not at all.

I hope this compendium of expert views is of some benefit and, if nothing else, promotes further thought and shared discussion on the matter.

Two final points: In the public sector, we buy the vast majority of our works, goods and services from the private sector. More than a third, and in some cases more than three quarters, of budget expenditure is with third parties.

Surely, it is wise to understand how we spend that money and how we could do so more effectively. This may demand adopting best practice from the private sector.

I am not arrogant enough to think, nor profess, that all of our words are pearls of wisdom (though some are). Every reader will know some, much, many or indeed all of the skills, tools and techniques we have discussed. It is presented in such a way that you may 'pick and mix' and, it is hoped, discover some 'golden nuggets' to inform, challenge or create debate in your commercial operations. I do hope so.

This publication has been written by 18 contributors from across our business and beyond with over 400 years combined experience, having worked both in and for the public sector that we are proud to continue to serve. I am immensely proud of all of them and indeed all the team who are the 'very best of the best'.[2] I do hope our thoughts are helpful and insightful.

> *'Here is Edward Bear, coming downstairs now, bump, bump, bump, bump, on the back of his head, behind Christopher Robin. It is, as far as he knows, the only way of coming downstairs, but sometimes he feels that there is another way, if only he could stop bumping for a moment and think of it.'*
>
> AA Milne
> *Winnie the Pooh* (1926)

2. *Top Gun*. (1985) – who doesn't like *Top Gun*!?

Ian McPherson OBE BEM FCIPS

Chief Operating Officer
4C Associates Ltd

Part 1 | Be Commercially Aware

Chapter 1 | Know Yourself and Your Organisation

'The key is not how to do things right, but to do the right things.'
Peter Drucker, Austrian-American management consultant, educator and author (1909–2005)

If we were to create something like a *Procurement Catechism*, an organisation – and, in turn, everyone in it – should at least be able to ask and answer the first two questions about itself: Who are we? And why do we exist?

It is that insightful nugget that is characteristically placed on the 'about us' page of an organisation's website that gives the thumbnail sketch. Better ones may also give a timeline (*when*) of the *who* and *why* that led to the organisation's creation. Companies and charities may call these elements objects. Though not physical, they are at least tangible because they help to define the purpose of the institution. And it is the extension of that understanding of the foundations of an organisation – be that company, charity or government department – that should permeate and inform all of the decisions that an organisation makes along the way, including what it buys and why. For example, a housing association or charity – there are several such as Shelter – established in the wake of the furore created by the 1966 Ken Loach documentary, *Cathy Come Home*, may have moved on commercially, but has never forgotten its *raison d'être*, which was to address the causes and consequences of homelessness.

By extension, many organisations will have built upon those foundations with the creation of a set of values, goals and strategies that may be very useful tools and a starting point for understanding what the organisational objectives are, how you – as an individual – can contribute to them, and what you need to achieve the aims of the business. This should help underpin everything that you do. It sounds like this should be a simple exercise of familiarisation but a study by Kaplan and North, 2005, revealed that 95 per cent of employees didn't understand how their day-to-day activities contributed to the strategy of their organisations, underscoring how important it is that the objectives are understood and applied.

Of course, it would be pure folly to cling slavishly to a set of values that have become outdated and need to be adapted or expanded to suit the present day. Think of the proliferation of businesses created during the Victorian era to address the age's preoccupation with digestion. Many, including some of today's biggest names and their products, like Coca-Cola, Kellogg's (*Corn Flakes*) and McVitie's (*Digestives*), were created to improve health and promote 'regularity' but today they and their products would be seen as very mainstream and not necessarily health-driven (though it does bring a whole new meaning to the origin of the expression '*fast moving consumer goods*').

Meanwhile, some businesses have held steadfastly to their beliefs. Take The Entertainer toy store: In 1981, a devout young Christian couple bought one shop in Buckinghamshire and created a concept which has grown into the UK's largest toy retailer with more than 170 stores and which is a familiar sight in many metropolitan shopping centres. Without analysing what led to its success – which was, no doubt, the usual synergy of smart decision-making complemented by serendipity – what resonates is that, to this day and decades on, its owners have stuck to their principles. The Entertainer does not open on a Sunday. Landlords of shopping centres have taken the retailer to court to force it, like their other tenants, to open seven days a week but it has always refused – sticking to its guns and never compromising on its original Christian sabbatical values. That, alone, is not why the company is a success story, but the fact that it never lost sight of who it was can only have helped.

On the flipside, a government body set up to provide training decided to build some accommodation for its trainees, which seemed to be an activity ancillary to its purpose. But, over time, it expanded its offering by making its hotel available to businesses and the general public for conferences and weddings. The decision was, no doubt, based on the good commercial intention of maximising revenue from rooms that weren't being used at the weekend. Unfortunately, the departure from its purpose not only placed the body in potential *ultra vires* territory but was also a commercial misstep. The organisation's roots and strengths were in delivering courses and it was well-equipped to make the purchases and commercial decisions that were associated with them; its investments, however, around conferences and weddings were less sound, because they strayed too far from its purpose, and the model proved unsustainable. It didn't help that the venue was very remote and the former military base it used proved a less than photogenic backdrop for the wedding album!

Knowing your organisation – and putting that at the forefront of your decisions and your contribution – is essential, as the above example illustrates. If the story of a chance meeting between President John F Kennedy and a NASA employee in 1961 is to be believed, a janitor who was mopping the floor responded to a query, from the President, about what he was doing with: *'I'm helping put a man on the moon!'* The tale may be apocryphal, but it emphasises the importance of seeing the big picture, although that also needs to be broken down. Part of that exercise, of knowing your organisation, is understanding yourself, your colleagues and the external factors that affect you. The sum of all these parts is critical in being able to think commercially and in helping the organisation to deliver against its objectives.

Knowing yourself and your organisation improves commercial thinking

Once the ethos of the organisation has been absorbed – and this should always be a compulsory part of any induction process for joiners – individuals are, perhaps, better placed to attempt to achieve the aims. Thinking commercially is about thinking in the best interests of the organisation's desired outcomes and ensuring that everyone in the organisation is on board with that too. As that is a group effort, it's essential to know yourself, your colleagues and the influences on the organisation, including those reflected in the corporate behaviours – an element of interconnectivity that is further examined in Chapter 2 – 'Be Connected'.

There are several steps that you can take, both as an individual, and as part of a team, that will help bring the concept of the 'intelligent customer' to life. You need to become an intelligent customer both personally and collectively, not only within the organisation, but across the supply chain. An intelligent customer must not only understand the organisation and its needs but should have the requisite technical knowledge of the suppliers, supply chain and the goods, services or works being provided by them to specify requirements competently and manage their delivery. This self-awareness does not just happen; it needs to be nurtured and developed through a series of phases.

First, get to know yourself

In the working environment, you need to know *who* you are dealing with. Therefore, the best person to start with is...*you*. If you don't fully understand what *your* motivations and characteristics are, you stand little chance of *objectively* assessing others and understanding what might motivate them and how to get the best out of your work with them, particularly if you want to understand if their thinking is commercial and open to entrepreneurial innovation, or merely procedural.

This is not about the meaning of life or consideration of your very existence. You just need to take some time to be sure about what your motivations are and to recognise your own traits. Recognise how *you* think and how *you* like things to be. Consider how you might think differently from others you work with and how they are from you. You can then stand back and consider, as objectively as possible, how your motivations and characteristics could influence your decisions and your approach to work situations and tasks. Through this exercise, as a bonus by-product, you might even identify how you might make some personal changes. (That's certainly what happens to most of us.)

There are plenty of online and print resources available to help you with this. On motivations, *What Motivates Me: Put Your Passions to Work* by Adrian Gostick and Chester Elton[3] is a good place to start. The real purpose of that book is identifying what motivates you and then aligning your work accordingly. That's great, of course, if you have the luxury of being able to choose what you would like to do or even pick and choose which bits of the job you want to do. Nevertheless, that book is well worth a read for the first part alone – it presents simple methods to identify what your motivations are.

Quite rightly, that book commands a hefty price tag. It's a well-researched and presented work by world-renowned experts. But you might not yet be convinced to make that particular investment or may not have access to a library from which you can borrow a copy for free (*and maybe this is secretly telling about some of your motivations already!*)

You must have a decent handle on what motivates you – maybe how your motivations impact how you go about your work and even how others might perceive you. If you do not think commercially, even unintentionally, then others will more than likely follow suit. You are in a position of leadership as a result of your role in the procurement chain of your organisation when it buys goods or services or builds things (or all three) and the way you display your thoughts will influence others.

And now, get to know your colleagues

Now that you are starting to get a feel for your own motivations, it is time to look at those of your colleagues. As is the case for personal motivations, there are many resources in the public domain that can help. Try to put yourself in the place of key colleagues, using what you know about them to try to understand their motivations. You may even know their personality type because you both took a personality test together at one time, or because if you cast your mind back to the years BC (*Before COVID-19*), you actually met or socialised with them – there is nothing more insightful about behaviour.

3. Gostick, A. and Elton, C. (2014) *What Motivates Me: Put Your Passions to Work.*

To understand your colleagues, why they act as they do and how to work with them for the best results, the Deloitte Business Chemistry[4] '20 questions' tool is also excellent. Give it a try. If all else fails, you could even think about asking them in general conversation.

So, you know who you are and who they are – what about the organisation?

By now, just by doing some structured thinking about you and your colleagues using external tools, you will already be getting to know a significant part of your organisation – namely the people within it. To round this off and to get back to where we started, you can now look at both external and internal influences on your organisation and develop a deeper understanding of why it behaves as it does. You might, for example, consider undertaking a PESTLE analysis (the Chartered Institute of Personnel and Development provides excellent free resources on this subject[5]). Now, it is hoped, that you are aligned with the organisation's objectives, let's think about what it – as an enterprise – needs to consider.

Knowing the organisation

Having looked at what breathed life into your organisation and how the human capital is sustaining it, it is a good point of principle to interrogate any procurement exercise with a familiar interrogative toolkit much beloved by journalists and appropriate to any investigatory procedure: *Who? What? Where? When? Why?*

Who (is it you are there to serve)? What (is it that you are there to deliver)? Where? When? Why? And 'how' will the contract deliver against the organisation's vision, mission and goals?

So – first – it's important that the organisation has a vision or philosophy – some might use the terminology goals, values, aims – that helps to define it. These mantras may, of course, evolve over time, but let's take an example of a company that, say, 'specialises in the provision of commercial *support*, challenge and delivery, working *with*… (its) clients to deliver *lasting improvements*.' There are a few things to unpack here semantically, but what you might notice is the emphasis on '*commercial support*' rather than '*commercial services*' and the '*working with*' rather than '*working for*' clients; the distinction in language – in the former *support;* the latter *with* – is imperative and suggests a collaborative

4. Deloitte. (2021) *Business Chemistry: Using science to improve the art of business relationships*. Available at: https://www2.deloitte.com/us/en/pages/operations/solutions/business-chemistry.html
5. CIPD. (2021) *PESTLE analysis*. Available at: https://www.cipd.co.uk/knowledge/strategy/organisational-development/pestle-analysis-factsheet#gref

approach with the client, rather than an arm's-length relationship. The '*lasting improvements*' tells you this is an organisation that doesn't just want to cut and run from business relationships but wants its actions to have an enduring impact on those it serves. In turn, it is probably an organisation that is looking to uphold those values in the supply chain that serves it too. This should tell you something about the ethos of the organisation and, perhaps, we should tell you that this is a guiding principle of the organisation behind the creation of this book.

Of course, it cuts both ways. Just as it is important to model your own values, it may be worth interrogating the visions of the suppliers whose goods, services or works you intend to use. This is especially so if, when you are buying goods, services or works you are keen to incorporate metrics such as social value into your requirements – a theme examined later in this book – so that you can identify suitable contenders.

If you truly know your organisation and the standards and culture that are articulated in its vision, it follows that you have a standard against which you can measure all your activities. Of course, it equally applies that if you don't fundamentally know your own organisation, you won't be in a position to know that the contracts that you are putting in place are delivering what you want. It may be worth taking some time, at the outset, to consider the following:

1. How well is your procurement aligned with the corporate strategy and plan? For example, if sustainability is a major element of your business or delivering social value is high on your corporate agenda, but your procurement team and suppliers are only chasing lowest price, there is a clear mismatch that needs to be addressed.
2. Do the suppliers know your organisation's goals and objectives and how are they helping you to deliver them?
3. Are your organisation's corporate values written anywhere and are your suppliers aligned with them?
4. Do you know what the priority areas are for your business?
5. Have your priority areas changed recently because of internal or external factors?
6. Do you need to realign your own ways of working and values to the current situation?

If your organisation is in the public sector, the legislation underpinning your body's creation will also set out your statutory duties and powers. You should have these at the forefront of your mind when you are making commercial decisions. They are complemented by a raft of obligations and guidance from government that should inform your behaviours in every activity including and beyond procurement. While they are mandatory or discretionary for different parts of the public sector, they may also be best practice for the private sector too. So, consider:

1. Positively discriminating in favour of a particular disadvantaged or under-represented group in your tendering. The Public Sector Equality Duty goes beyond the requirement not to discriminate on the basis of age, disability, gender reassignment, marriage and civil partnership, pregnancy and maternity, race, religion or belief, sex and sexual orientation. Section 149 of the Equality Act 2010 (the EA 2010) actively requires public authorities to 'advance' the causes of those that are disadvantaged, so maybe, that is something that you should consider in terms of the suppliers that are available to you in the selection process and tailor a tender to make that a consideration. There is, of course, a fine line to be trodden so that suppliers are still treated fairly and transparently.
2. Thinking about socioeconomic inequalities. The onus here is less than 'advancing' but public authorities are told to have 'due regard' to the disadvantage in exercising their functions, under Section 1 of the EA 2010. While 'duly considering' is a lower standard than 'advancing' it is, nevertheless, a prompt to evaluate and factor in considerations in your procurement. It might even be your justification for insisting that suppliers pay all their staff or their suppliers, in turn, theirs, the Living Wage.
3. Earmarking contracts of a lower value by region or category. Central government can (though local government may not – Section 17 of the Local Government Act 1988) earmark lower value contracts to tackle economic inequality, create new businesses, jobs and skills, as well as increasing supply chain resilience, encouraging entrepreneurship, and attracting new entrants to government markets, favouring SMEs and VCSEs. Under the UK-wide PPN 11/20, this can be done county- or UK-wide, but not by home country but, if you're in Wales (WPPN 05/21), you can specify regions, for example North Wales.

Making a difference

A company's vision should be about what it hopes to achieve in the future but that is probably something it needs to do without losing sight of its beginnings. As the late, great author Maya Angelou said: 'You can't really know where you are going until you know where you have been.' An organisation's values should, by definition, be positive. This is because the meaning of value (explored further in Chapter 11 – 'Manage Value') is something of worth, and that can also apply to even the smallest random acts of kindness, as we discover in Chapter 16 – 'Be a

Good Citizen'. There are several examples of successful individuals who were once homeless. Oracle billionaire tycoon Larry Ellison is one of them, and he is among those who has ploughed some of his vast fortune back into good causes that match some corporate ideals: conservation, education, health and development.

As an organisation, it is just as important to remember where you started – be that as a start-up or an SME – and remember that your commercial decisions and procurement activity can affect organisations who are in the shoes you once wore when you started out years ago. Use those experiences to drive how you go about doing business, be that encouraging entrepreneurship or giving an up-and-coming organisation, perhaps from a deprived neighbourhood, an opportunity. You must know yourself, your staff, and how they can direct the energy that legacy brings in the supply chain. You should inspire your suppliers to do that wisely too.

We began by saying that the starting point for all organisations should be understanding who they are and why they exist, so let us turn to ourselves.

Who? We, a newly acquired subsidiary of 4C Associates, began life in 2015 when a former Lieutenant-Colonel of the British Army, now twice honoured by The Queen, set up a company. **Why?** To capitalise on a career of public service so he and colleagues could use their expertise to consult in the public sector, from which sprung the mantra: 'Private by Head, Public by Heart.' The lessons from that journey are our legacy to you.

Chapter 2 | Be Connected

'No man is an island entire of itself; every man is a piece of the continent, a part of the main.'

John Donne, English metaphysical poet (1572 – 1631)

This chapter very much builds on Chapter 1 – 'Know yourself and your organisation'. Having recently moved into a consultancy role I realise more than ever the importance of my past and current relationships, but whether you are working at director level or starting in your first public sector procurement role, don't forget to keep yourself connected! I see being connected as the 'glue' that holds all the pieces of the jigsaw together to give me a complete picture and deliver the very best outcomes.

This chapter will focus on the importance of the connections for procurement professionals. A good starting point is to understand the importance of doing a

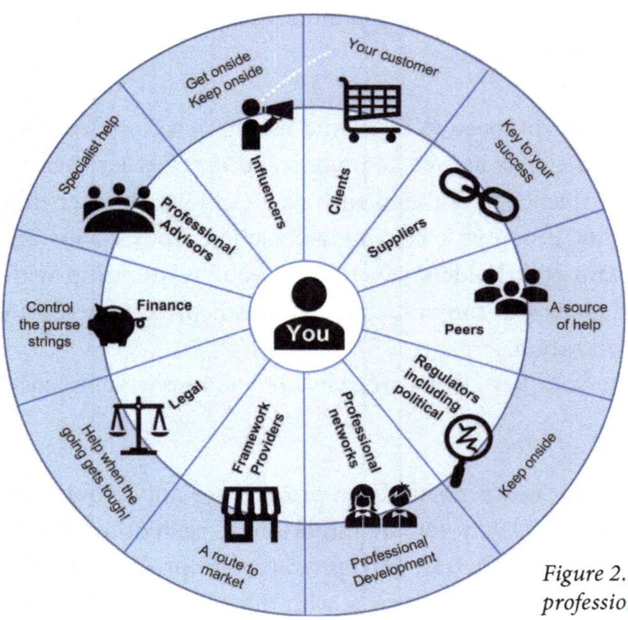

Figure 2.1. Public procurement professional stakeholder map.

stakeholder map. Whilst this is often talked about, most individuals, me included, would admit that it is something they do on starting in a new job or project, but not necessarily something they have gone back to and refreshed regularly. Whilst there are numerous stakeholder maps, the one in Figure 2.1 reflects my experience of who it is important to engage with both internally and externally and why they are important to the success of you, the organisation you work for and, ultimately the end-customer who benefits from the outcomes of your collective work.

The stakeholder map is split into segments with the inner segments defining who you need to connect with and the outer segment explaining why you want to stay connected. It can be used to think about how you stay connected, regardless of your seniority, both with colleagues within the procurement function, and also with those who interface with it.

Let's imagine you have just started in a new procurement role in the public sector. How do you identify who to stay connected with and why? Or maybe you have actually found some time to reflect on how you are performing in an established role? Where are your relationships working well, which ones need a refresh, and which ones are you unsure why you are even bothering with?

In this chapter we will explain a little more about the importance of each segment and give examples of how they interconnect. All the stakeholders are important to some degree and their relative importance will change over time, but it is likely that some will always be the top of your list.

Here's why you need to build and maintain those relationships:

Clients – those who sit between you and the end-customers, delivering the final outcomes that satisfy them

As a procurement professional you need to build and maintain a close working relationship with your direct clients as well as understanding whether there is someone who has strong influence over them, such as a Cabinet Member in a Local Authority or a tenants' group in a housing association. Your clients are arguably the most important stakeholders you have as your relationship with them will influence how successful individual procurement projects are, and your reputation in the organisation.

So, after finding out who your key clients are, why are you important to each other?

1. The consequences of poor procurement from projects are not an outcome either of you want and that is why you are important to each other. When public sector procurement is reactive, with procurement projects rushed, with very little time for pre-market research, with the quickest rather than

the optimal approach chosen, the outcomes are generally poor. The key to avoiding this is that strong relationship with your clients to understand their priorities and develop a joint pipeline of upcoming procurement projects, ideally over a two-year horizon. This will allow you to do market research, and you can talk to peers about what has worked in the past and equally importantly what hasn't and why. Chapter 10 – 'Plan for success, prepare for failure' explores this in more detail.

2. As a procurement professional you are most likely to be successful if you have early visibility of projects, so you need to ensure your clients always think of you as the first contact when they have a project, rather than at a point when the order nears finalisation and procedures say your approval is needed. In this situation you simply won't add any value. So, your objective is that clients come to you because they see you as a value-adding partner, not because the procedures instruct them to. You need to understand the *outcome* your client is trying to achieve, rather than the specific *output* that they have traditionally demanded. If you understand the end-customer need that drives the requirement, you are more likely to offer the best solution (perhaps an innovative outsourcing rather than repeat short-term provision of consumables etc).
3. Your clients are likely to have specific priorities for any procurement you support them on, so the first thing I always ask is what they are. Unless you understand them it will be really difficult to make a difference and be seen by your client as an enabler rather than a blocker, a common perception when poorly informed or obsolete legacy procurement decisions are questioned.
4. Inevitably things will go wrong on projects and you are less likely to get into the blame game if you have a strong partnership established. You are more likely to solve the issue together and both learn from the experience.

Suppliers

If you are responsible for a particular category of spend, one of your first tasks will be to understand who your key suppliers are. Prior to engaging with your supplier account manager for the first time it is essential to use some of the established analytical tools such as Supply Positioning Analysis (buyer perspective of priorities) and Supplier Preferencing Analysis (supplier view). These will help you understand the supplier's perspective of *you* as a customer. This tool will help you understand where your focus should be and who you need to connect with as a priority, which may not always be the supplier with the highest spend – it could, for example, be the supplier of an item or service critical to the success of a project.

It will help you frame what your objectives should be from the relationship. Whilst this chapter will not explore either tool in any depth, the diagram below provides a summary of the four main types of relationship. It will help you decide what actions you should take depending on your suppliers' perspective of your relationship under a typical supplier preferencing model (Figure 2.2).

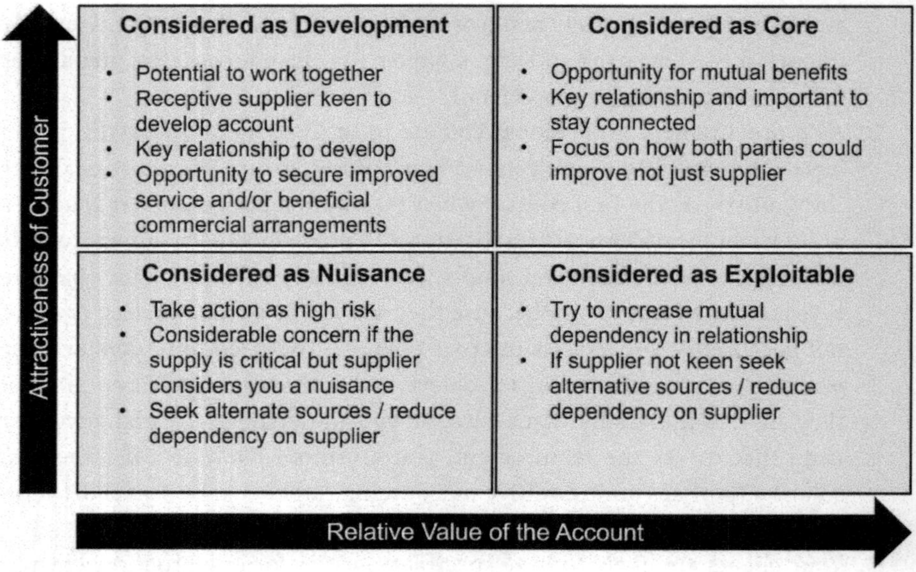

Figure 2.2. Supplier preferencing analysis.

Using the four-box model in Figure 2.2, once you know where you are from your supplier's viewpoint you can start the engagement. Make sure that it is the Account Manager you are focusing your attention on rather than the salesperson who may have been the first point of contact with the organisation. The reason this is important is the salesperson will be driven by sales volume whereas the Account Manager has scope to make strategic improvements to the account.

If you are in the nuisance box then you are likely to have little opportunity to engage meaningfully with your Account Manager and your approach should either be based on reducing any dependency you have with the supplier or trying to make your account more attractive to them.

If you are in the exploitable box for your supplier, your aim should be to engage with your Account Manager to increase the attractiveness of your requirements to their business portfolio. If you can become core to its business it is likely to increase the level of service it will offer you. If it becomes clear that your engagement is not successful in achieving this, then reducing your dependency on this supplier becomes the priority because you are likely to see on-going price increases with little commitment to improvements.

The final two boxes offer more opportunity to work together for mutual benefit but before you start this consider what you, and importantly, your clients want to achieve from the relationship in the future.

Peers

One key lesson I learnt quickly on taking up a role in the public sector is the willingness of peers to freely share information and examples of best practice. This is much less common in the private sector where my peers were often my direct competitors.

In the public sector collaboration is actively encouraged. In some departments the amount of collaborative procurement you have done with peers is considered a measure of your success. My own experience was that developing and staying connected with a trusted group of peers was invaluable in terms of helping me to understand the sector I had joined in the shortest time possible.

Then, as that trust developed, collaborative endeavour became a great way to share ideas and understand what new approaches worked or not, and importantly, why.

If you have joined as a new procurement director with little past experience of your particular sector, your peers should be able to help you understand the landscape, the role of the regulators, professional networks and relevant framework providers. In return you will be able to contribute different approaches and experiences from your past roles that may not have been tried in that particular environment.

If you are a new procurement professional responsible for a particular category of spend, your peers should help you gain a better understanding of your particular markets and how they work with the public sector. In return, if you have recently joined from another part of the public or private sector, you can share your experience of the markets where you have worked. Try and do this in a humble way and be sensitive to a natural resistance to change – do not become a 'Wheneye', starting every discussion with 'When I was at…' implying that everything was done so much better there! Offer a balanced view supported by real evidence of benefits *and* risks. Remember, not all organisations will achieve the same benefits in different circumstances, and risks may be significantly larger. Your peers will also be able to share insights into relevant client and supplier engagement specific to your area as well as any collaborative initiatives or working groups you need to be aware of.

Working with your peers to achieve mutual benefit is a key and an enjoyable part of working in procurement in the public sector and if your relationships are developed and maintained it can be a free and very effective mutual consultancy service.

Regulators

If you are working in the public sector in procurement at director or head of procurement level you are likely to have some interface with external regulators and it is critical that you know who the regulators are, what their remit is and how they are likely to want to interface with you. The regulatory regime may be light touch with just a regulatory framework that you are required to work within, or it may be more hands-on with audits. Whichever form the regime takes, my approach is to be proactive and transparent in my relationship with the regulators to reduce uncertainty so they feel they have less of a need to intervene. As a procurement professional or service deliverer at any level, understanding the director's regulatory relationships not only enhances your own effectiveness and builds trust that your superiors and peers will have in you, but also allows you to pre-empt nugatory effort pursuing solutions that will be constrained or even rejected later in the process. Engage with your senior leadership and discuss their attitudes, relationships and approaches with regulators. This way, you can work within their personal bounds as well as those of external regulators.

Professional networks

Regardless of what level you are, it is worth finding out what professional networks exist and looking at the benefits of staying connected across the wider profession. There are likely to be a wide range of networks you could participate in so check with others in the team which networks they are already linked with, be selective and find out which is the best for you. As mentioned previously, collaboration is actively encouraged in the public sector and these professional networks are an invaluable source of information, personal and professional development and opportunities. Many of them have policy forums and can, on occasion, provide a unified and powerful voice to regulators and wider government on guidance and legislation that impacts procurement, such as the Public Contracts Regulations. They help you to keep abreast of constantly changing public procurement policies in areas such as social value requirements. These professional networks are also a platform for change.

The networks could include:

1. Professional bodies such as the Chartered Institute of Procurement and Supply (CIPS) or World Commerce & Contracting (formerly the International Association for Contract & Commercial Management – IACCM).
2. Professional networks for procurement professionals in the public sector you work in.
3. Regional groupings of procurement professionals.
4. Public sector buying organisations who often operate support networks for their members.

Framework providers

There are many providers of framework agreements to the public sector. Inevitably, the quality of each agreement varies, but they are a facility that you need to be aware of as a procurement professional. Do not focus solely on the frameworks set up specifically for your sector but also understand others that you may be able to access.

To get the most out of these arrangements I recommend you actively engage with the framework providers to help influence the shape of any relevant future agreements they create. After all, you are best placed to understand what works and doesn't and what best suits your needs.

When thinking about how you interface with framework providers, go back to your supplier positioning and supplier preferencing analysis. Look at any relationships you have in the nuisance or exploitable box that might be addressed by you using a framework agreement to secure those goods or services. This could lead to you becoming part of a relationship that is either in the development or core box. In my experience some of the framework providers do not update their range of agreements to reflect changes in the market in a timely manner. If a new collaborative framework agreement could help you, it is a real opportunity for both you and your peers to build and shape better framework agreements.

Legal and finance

You will want to stay connected and build relationships with all relevant internal colleagues. In my experience as a procurement professional, legal and finance are key first areas to build your relationships with.

As a director of procurement or senior procurement professional, having a good relationship with individuals in legal is an essential step to getting proactive practical advice on new legislation, and developing agreements that clearly set out both parties' responsibilities, but also reactively when things go wrong. For example, if you receive a challenge from an unsuccessful bidder, getting early and trusted advice from legal colleagues can often allow you to address the challenge effectively. Working as a team, you may be able to dismiss the challenge successfully and even sometimes amicably! Alternatively, you can recognise early that you have made an error and address the problem before you start digging the hole even deeper. If you haven't already built relationships with your legal advisers, it's not a great time to start when you are faced with a legal challenge from an aggrieved supplier (See Chapter 12 – 'Use Legal Counsel Wisely').

As a procurement professional, you are likely to have multiple interfaces with your colleagues in finance. As a director of procurement, you will want to build your personal and professional relationships with the finance director. Your aim is to ensure both the finance team and the Board (where the finance director will have significant influence) fully understand the contribution that procurement can make to financial savings, and importantly, to meeting the organisation's objectives such as operational outcomes and sustainability. Building and maintaining a close relationship with the finance team is unlikely to save you from facing the same scrutiny on your own budget and pressure to reduce costs as others across the organisation. It might, however, create opportunities to agree alternative approaches where you can maintain or even invest in the procurement service to deliver greater savings for the organisation, as a whole. Experience indicates that is an easier sell if you have already developed the relationship with senior stakeholders in finance and proved the added value of what you and your team do before any budget crisis hits.

As a senior procurement professional, those relationships are again important at an operational level when you want help with financial analysis of a company, or shorter payment terms to secure a better deal.

Professional advisers (consultants)

As a procurement professional you are likely to help procurement consultants. You could potentially engage consultants to assist the procurement team directly in specialist areas where you need their expertise.

Some procurement professionals may have concerns about building relationships with consultants and professional advisers based on conflicts over having to be transparent and independent in any future procurement exercise. This should not be seen as a barrier to building a close relationship, as long as it remains professional. My experience of using professional advisers is that if you are clear on what outcomes or outputs you need and there is mutual trust between the two parties, they will often provide a valuable contribution. I have, however, seen consultants engaged in some areas where they are given vague briefs and are subsequently poorly managed. One of the unfortunate consequences is that the consultant naturally exploits and expands scope to meet the need the consultant perceives rather than the one you need, and unless challenged this can lead to poor-use of taxpayers' money.

Having and using the right connections as shown in the stakeholder map will help you as a procurement professional ensure your organisation gets the most from any consultancy engagements it enters into, and some examples are detailed below:

1. Engage with your clients and key influencers early through the connections network to identify the likely future requirement for consultants well before they are actually needed. This will give you the early visibility to help you to influence the specification and possible procurement options rather than

being introduced to the consultant on arrival, as I have experienced in the past!

2. Find out if anyone in your peer network has undertaken a similar consultancy project previously. Explore whether you can use the consultant's experiences with this, potentially even avoiding the need of the consultant but at least learning from previous successes (and mistakes).
3. Find out through your peer network and framework providers if there is a suitable framework you can utilise to provide the desired outcome.
4. Check where the relationship with a consultant is likely to rest on the supply preferencing matrix and consider what risks and opportunities this brings. This is especially relevant if your client or key influencers are recommending a particular supplier or suppliers capable of doing the work.
5. Use your network of consultancy supplier contacts to identify other potential providers who could bid for the work to ensure you achieve value for money.
6. In terms of the procurement of consultants the key points for me are defining:
    i. Clear outputs/outcomes.
    ii. Clear agreements on transfer and ownership of knowledge during the assignment.
    iii. What benefits are expected and when.
    iv. What constitutes the end of the defined assignment.
    v. Who is responsible for managing the consultancy relationship.
7. As a procurement professional you also need to provide support managing the resulting contracts and be brave enough to challenge the contract owner if the work is expanding beyond the original remit. There may be a valid and reasonable case to do so, but it should be captured and regulated by the procurement process.
8. Most importantly are they putting any fees at risk of achieving *outcomes*? And if not, why not?

Lastly, remember your role to challenge if a procurement is required at all. Always consider if there is an internal resource that should be used; just because you are paying for external advice, does not mean it is better than professional advice from your colleagues.

Influencers

Every organisation I have ever worked in has had people who are key influencers and have the ear of the Chief Executive. As a new director of procurement or senior procurement professional you need to identify who these individuals are and prioritise building and maintaining a good professional relationship with them.

A key objective will be for you to demonstrate to them the value that their contribution, you and the wider procurement team can make to operational output and customer outcomes. This will increase your chances of being involved in key projects in a timely manner and facilitate you using them as a sounding board for your future initiatives. As key influencers within the organisation, they are also likely to be aware of who might potentially block any initiatives you might have and help you to pre-empt or overcome these challenges.

In conclusion, enjoy building the professional procurement jigsaw that you are going to hang on the wall when it is finished and think of your connections as the glue that keeps the full picture together.

Chapter 3 | Know What is Really Needed – ROAD© Part 1

'If you don't know what you want you will probably never get it.'
Oliver Wendell Holmes, Jr. Former Associate
Justice of the US Supreme Court (1841–1935)

Benjamin Franklin is credited with having told us that, *'failing to prepare is preparing to fail'* – a message so popular it has multiple attributions and is a recurring theme of this book. It is one of many well-known and frequently used quotes, extolling the importance of planning in the execution of any task or activity, and there is a generally accepted logic, in most disciplines, that an appropriate amount of planning is a beneficial thing.

In procurement terms, taking time at the pre-planning stage to take a radical and critical view of the current arrangements, ensuring that the true cost of procurement is understood, and genuinely understanding the market with which you are engaging, significantly increases the chances of conducting a successful procurement. This accepted wisdom does not, however, necessarily find its way into day-to-day custom and practice.

The complexity and legal requirements of procurement regulations, mean that engaging in procurement can require a significant investment from public sector organisations, not only in terms of the monetary cost, but also as a result of the resources that are necessary to ensure the process is followed correctly. Unfortunately, whilst important, this focus on process and unthinking compliance can leave little additional space or energy for those vital qualitative considerations which have the potential to make the crucial difference between 'good' procurement and just 'well regulated' procurement. In fact, lack of time to devote to adequate preparation is often the main enemy of effective procurement.

Another challenge is the perceived risk of over-planning. We are not, as far as I know, a species of soothsayers and, by and large, we cannot guarantee a future course of events, particularly when in many procurement projects there are multiple variables in play, or if we are trying to look many months or even years into the future. If, as Prussian Field Marshal Helmuth von Moltke suggested, '*no plan survives first contact with the enemy*,' then, surely, there is a danger that time spent preparing can be wasted, if carefully crafted plans unravel, as soon as they are put into practice, or are followed slavishly but fail to deliver the desired outcomes. The planning process is therefore more important than the actual plan in some respects; as a minimum, it tells you where you are now, and where you want to be. The evolving plan will successfully navigate you between those two points, but only if you actually monitor your progress and maintain vision of the end aim or outcome.

These tensions are ubiquitous and are as relevant to public sector procurements as they are to any other project or endeavour. The secret to getting the right balance between planning and action, particularly in the early stages of a procurement project, is to be really clear about the sequence in which decisions need to be made and by applying challenge at the right time in the decision cycle.

One way of approaching it from the outset is to consider the '*6 Rights*'[6].

1. **Right Product**

in the

2. **Right Place**

at the

3. **Right Time**

at the

4. **Right Price**

of the

5. **Right Quality**

and in the

6. **Right Quantity**

Although seemingly obvious, it is the first of these requirements – *the importance of having the right product* – that is often given insufficient priority in the early stages.

To assist with this, MCP2, a subsidiary of 4C, developed ROAD© – a simple but effective framework to assist organisations with the pre-planning phase of complex procurements. Initially conceived by MCP2's founder, Ian McPherson OBE BEM

6. Some texts quote the '5 Rights' and include the 'Right Supplier' in the list, but in our experience, if you have the 6 Rights listed above, the Right Supplier will be found.

FCIPS, the ROAD© approach was first presented and accepted at the International Purchasing and Supply Education and Research Association (IPSERA) Annual Conference in Wiesbaden in 2009. In more than a decade since then, it has seen constant operational use, enhancing pre-procurement planning, and consistently enabling the most appropriate procurement strategy to be better identified.

ROAD© is an adaptable and fully scalable six-stage process summarised in Figure 3.1.

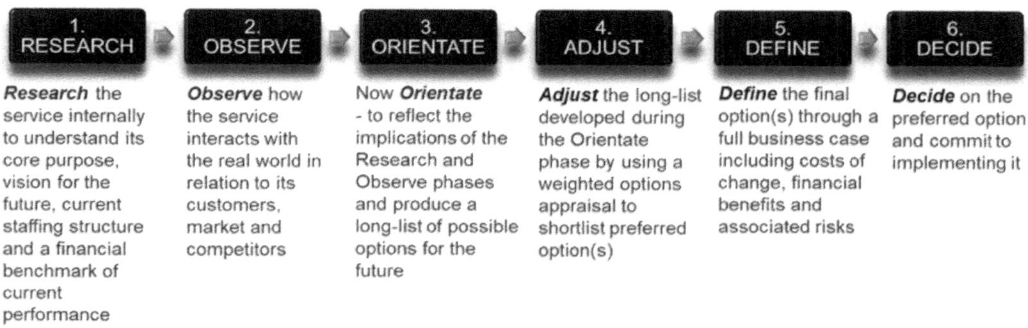

Figure 3.1. The ROAD© methodology.

The approach provides a framework for structuring and organising the pre-planning stage of a procurement, or in some cases to determine whether a procurement is necessary at all. Due in part to the regulatory framework of modern-day procurement, and the popularity of certain approaches, there is often little or no consideration given to which of the competitive tendering processes is most appropriate, or if a tendering process is necessary at all.

Adopting the ROAD© approach allows users to take a step back from the process itself and ask two key questions:

What are we trying to achieve, and what's the best way of achieving it?

Although much has been written about the downfalls and constraints of overly prescriptive procurement procedures, often there is little inherently wrong with the process itself, rather it is too often the case that a particular procurement approach is used in the wrong circumstances, or with insufficient pre-procurement planning.

The proper use of ROAD© to determine when and how best to procure, has frequently allowed its users to identify the most appropriate procurement approach. It can significantly improve the potential for successful business and commercial outcomes from any subsequent procurement activity.

The first ROAD© stage is to **Research** the requirements of the project, in order to define an Operational Statement of Requirement (OSR). The activity in this stage focuses internally and considers what the organisation needs to achieve. This is not simply a case of saying, 'I want a new helicopter' or 'I want a new social care provider', but rather gaining a much wider understanding of what is required. It is often described as the 'What' stage as we are seeking to clarify: What outputs do the stakeholders want? What do they want to achieve by this project? What is essential to its success, and what is merely desirable? These answers should be considered carefully, but pragmatically, and explored and expressed in terms of outputs with time and cost constraints.

For example, at the outset, it might have been stated that it was vital for the helicopter to be purple, yet upon discovering that the difference between a blue and a purple helicopter is six more months and the costs quadrupling, you might be perfectly happy to have a blue helicopter. This stage results in an OSR which is the first expression of what is wanted – importantly, it is 'operational' at this stage because it may be refined as the process continues.

In the Research stage, we need to answer a number of key questions. Answering these questions enables you to develop a series of outputs which will collectively form a draft specification that can then be tested with the market, during the next stage of the process, namely the Observe stage.

What is our end goal – and do we all understand and agree on it?

The first element of the Research stage aims rapidly to establish a shared vision and common vocabulary for the procurement project as early as possible in its life cycle. It is usually kicked off with a stakeholder mapping exercise, during which

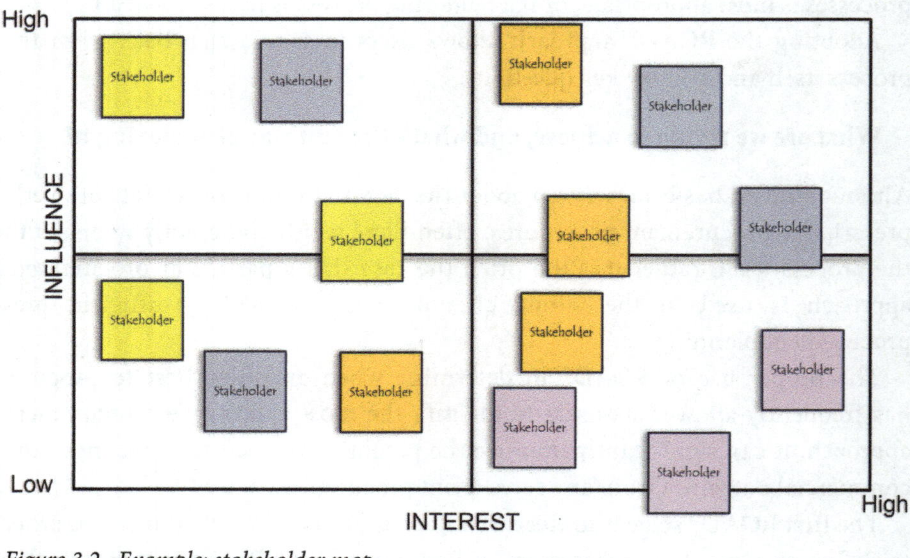

Figure 3.2. Example: stakeholder map.

the key stakeholders for the procurement are identified, grouped, and plotted on a simple stakeholder map.

Once stakeholders have been identified and mapped, it's important to engage with individual groups first, asking them to describe in simple terms how they see the product or service you are buying would work in practice. Ideally, you are looking to get them to draw this as a 'rich picture', taking up no more than one page, but, if this is not possible, then text-based outputs, capturing and grouping the key points on sticky notes, for example, can be just as effective.

The key point here is to start with a blank piece of paper and encourage unconstrained thinking. It is important, at this stage, that the groups focus on what they really need and what the best possible outcomes would look like for them, not what they think they can get or what they think will happen, based on what has happened before.

Figure 3.3. Example: A rich picture.

The output from this exercise, pictorial or otherwise, should include how the following relate to the product or service currently being bought:

1. Internal stakeholders
2. Potential delivery models
3. Customers of the service

Once the outputs from individual groups have been collected, it is important to bring the groups (or representatives from each group), together to agree on one common picture.

Involving all stakeholder groups at this early stage helps highlight potential problems with the procurement early enough in the process to design out or develop suitable mitigations for them and will predominantly save time and money, in the long run. The wide engagement, combined with the two-step approach, also helps overcome any unconscious bias within the team responsible for the procurement.

What are the desired outputs and outcomes of the procurement we are about to undertake?

In the second part of the Research stage, we take a deep dive into the functionality required from the product or service being procured. It is important to work through all the things the product or service might do and determine how important each element of potential functionality is to our stakeholders. More importantly, an objective assessment should be made of how important it is to the overall success of the product or service being procured.

The outputs from this exercise can be captured and prioritised through a simple MoSCoW analysis to determine, for each activity, whether it Must, Could, Should or Won't be included in your specification.

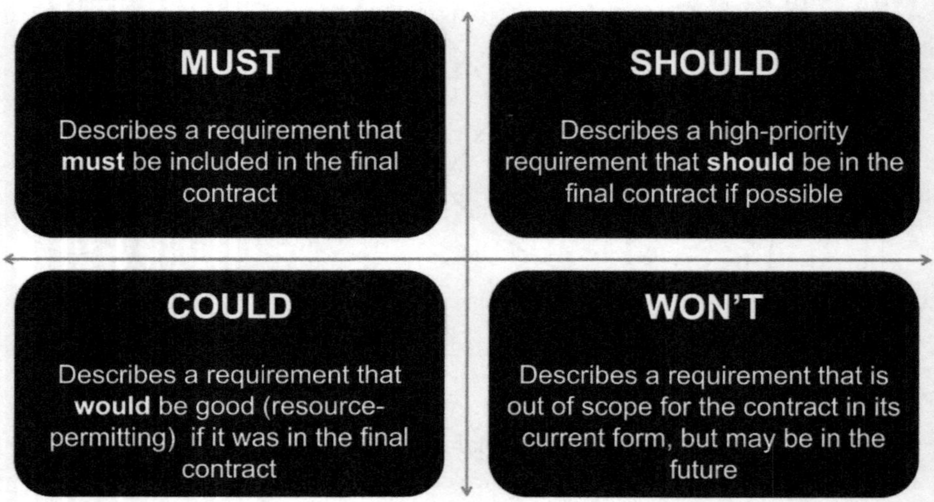

Figure 3.4. MoSCoW analysis.

What are the potential delivery models?

If a service is being procured, it is important at this stage to establish a comprehensive long-list of potential delivery models. Not so long ago, this would have been a pretty simple task, with public services being delivered via a relatively small number of traditional delivery models.

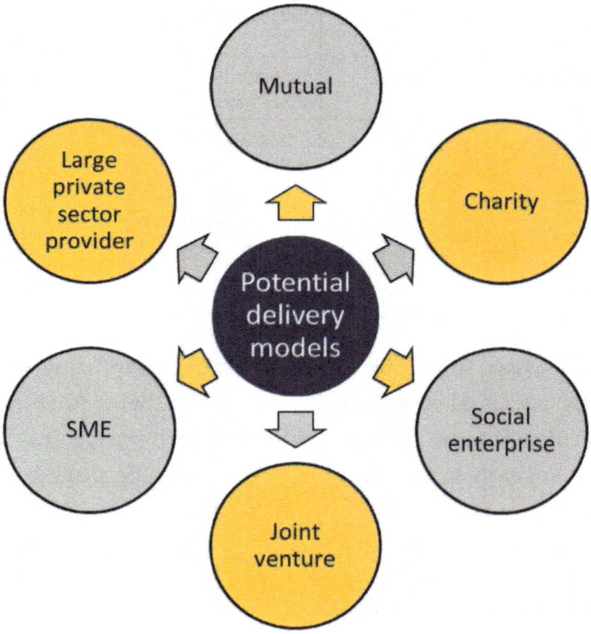

Figure 3.5. Established public sector delivery models.

However, in recent times, all that has changed. In the past few years, the UK public sector has faced extraordinary financial challenges while the pressure to make further budget reductions remains intense. These financial pressures, combined with increasing demand, rapid advancements in technology and changes in the way people expect to access and interact with services have opened a plethora of new and innovative delivery models to the public sector market.

Type	Example	Technology	Public sector role
Radical Restructuring	Buurtzorg	Professional Social Network	Radically empowering frontline staff
Augmenting Capacity of Public Service with Volunteers	GoodSAM	App integrated into public service	Working alongside volunteers
Government as Matchmaker	TrustonTap	Matchmaking Platform	Hosting or commissioning platform to connect people & organisations
Peer-to-peer support networks	Casserole Club	Peer-to-Peer Platform	Hosting or commissioning platform to connect people
(Digital) Social Innovation	Open Voice Factory	Open Source Software & Hardware	Partnering, incentivising signposting or incubating external organisations
Open Data Innovation	TfL Unified API	Open Data Portal	Releasing quality open data and providing support and context

Table 3.1. Six alternatives to traditional top-down public service delivery.[7]

The focus on this stage should be on identifying and capturing **all** of the potential delivery models that could be applicable to the service being procured. Whilst it may be possible to rule out some options legitimately at this stage, it is important not to narrow this list too early in the process. At this point, the aim is to identify as many potential options as possible, conducting an initial assessment of the pros and cons of each one, in order to establish its overall attractiveness to the organisation.

What is the current financial position?

The final task in the research stage is to confirm the baseline financial position of the current service, completing Table 3.2 (or equivalent) as accurately as possible.

	2 years ago (actual)	Last year (actual)	This year (budget)
Employees			
Marketing			
Premises			
Supplies/services			
Corporate overheads			
Other costs			
Total costs			
External income			
Net surplus/deficit			

Table 3.2. Example template: financial baseline.

7. Copeland, E. (2018) *Six alternatives to traditional top down public service delivery.* Available at: https://www.nesta.org.uk/blog/six-alternatives-traditional-top-down-public-service-delivery/

Research stage – the outputs and outcomes

By using these questions as a framework for your initial activity, at the end of the Research phase of the ROAD© review, you will:

1. Have secured **internal sign-off** for a **rich picture** of what you would like to buy, establishing a common vocabulary and setting out, at a high level, how the service relates to internal stakeholders and customers.
2. Know what you **must, should, could, and won't** have from the service you are buying.
3. Have considered the **potential delivery models** for the service you are buying and have formed a view on how attractive each model is to the organisation.
4. Hold clear financial data on the **current cost of the service** being bought.

In turn, these outputs will enable you to achieve the desired outcomes from this initial stage of the ROAD© process which are summarised below:

Output	Outcome
A 'rich picture' of the deal you are looking to develop.	Shared consensus on what the organisation is trying to achieve, an opportunity to identify problems early and a common vocabulary for discussing the procurement.
A MoSCoW analysis of outcomes and outputs that the organisation wants from the service.	The market response to the list of provisional outputs can be tested at the Observe phase to test whether they are viable.
A long list of potential delivery models and a clear picture of which ones are the most attractive to the organisation.	The market can be tested at the Observe phase as to whether such models are available or if the marketplace would be willing to deliver the service in question.
A financial baseline of the current cost of delivering the service.	The organisation can assess how much it is willing to pay for delivery of the service in question when it receives bids during the procurement process.

Table 3.3. Research stage outputs and outcomes.

In addition to establishing important internal clarity and cohesion around the procurement project, collectively, these outputs can now be used to draft the initial OSR. This will ensure that the key document achieves the right blend of accuracy, clarity and brevity for it to be used when the organisation engages with the market in the next stage of the ROAD© process: observing the market. This is taken forward in Chapter 5, 'Know the markets – ROAD© Part 2'.

Chapter 4 | Know Your Supply Chain

'There are no secrets to success. It is the result of preparation, hard work, and learning from failure.'

Colin Powell, late US statesman
and US Army four-star General

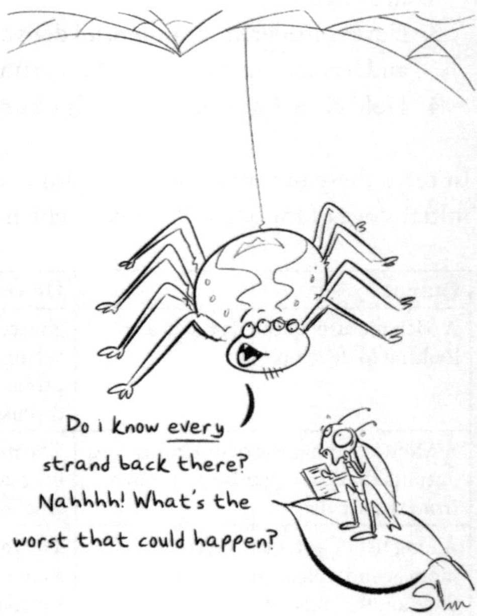

Chapter 13 – 'Spend Analysis' takes a retrospective look at spend within the supply chain, identifying which suppliers you used, how much you spent with them, where they are based, number of invoices and so on. This chapter takes a forward look at your suppliers and the supply chains that support them (i.e. those suppliers that **your** suppliers are dependent upon) in more depth and considers some of the thornier questions such as: does this supplier's ethical stance match our culture; how sustainable are they; are they profitable or are they at risk of collapse; if they, or an individual in their organisation, is involved in fraud is there a reputational impact on your organisation; how secure are their systems and processes or is there a risk that they may inadvertently lose data which is relevant to you as a customer? These are the sort of questions you need to understand before you contract with a supplier as well as during the lifetime of your relationship with that supplier and beyond. It is worth remembering that the supply chain does not just exist 'upstream' of you. You are an integral part of it, and it stretches end-to-end from secondary and tertiary tier suppliers right up to the end-customer or end-user (and sometimes in reverse back from them if a repair loop is incorporated).

The collapse of Carillion in 2018 is a perfect example of an organisation whose demise had serious ramifications for organisations, particularly in the public sector. Carillion was a leading player in the construction, facilities management and building sector and in 2017 was one of the UK Government's top 20 strategic suppliers providing services. It supported many public sector organisations including central and local government to hospitals, schools and housing associations. At the time it went bust it was working on around 420 UK public sector contracts. It was making a loss on a number of larger contracts, had significant debt and a poor debt/equity ratio, was renowned for bidding aggressively (and unsustainably) low to win work, was squeezing its suppliers by making them wait over 120 days for payment. It was known to have been in financial difficulties since 2015. The services Carillion provided to the public largely continued with other suppliers taking on the contracts (with a few major construction project exceptions), but the financial cost to the public sector of liquidation was estimated at £72 million.[8] This doesn't include the loss to suppliers and sub-contractors, impact on their 18,000 employees in the UK or the political, social and economic ramifications that its collapse had at the time.

If you were, or had been, a customer of Carillion's can you imagine the impact on your organisation and the additional workload, stress and reputational damage this would have had on your organisation? As a director did you, or would you have known or been made aware, three years before that there were financial issues with the company? As a procurement professional would you have made, or felt empowered to make, different decisions regarding evaluation if Carillion had bid significantly low for a project you were tendering? As a service/contract manager how would you have managed this situation, what contingencies would you have had in place?

It's all about knowing your supply chain.

Clearly not all suppliers are of equal importance to your organisation, nor will their success, creativity, issues or demise have the same impact on all of their client base. So, it is important to know which suppliers are the most important to your organisation. Understanding who you spend your money with is examined in Chapter 13 – 'Spend Analysis'. Leading organisations, however, will not only have undertaken (and continue to undertake) a spend analysis but they will also have access to the right insights, information and data about their suppliers in order to enrich their decision making and they will do this on a regular basis prior to, during and post tendering activities. Consider the following:

1. Do you know which suppliers are critical to your organisation and has your supply base or your contracts been analysed using the Kraljic Model?[9]
2. Do you know who the key movers and shakers are within your strategic categories of spend and in particular the up and coming small-to-medium enterprises (SMEs)?

---

8. Chapman, D. (2019) *Letter from the Official Receiver.* Available at: https://www.parliament.uk/globalassets/documents/commons-committees/work-and-pensions/Carillion/Letter-from-Official-Receiver-the-Insolvency-Service-re-Carillion-liquidation-update-30-October-2019.pdf
9. See Chapter 9 – 'Risk is inevitable – embrace it' which provides information on the Kraljic model in more detail.

3. Do you have appropriate controls in place to ensure that you are contracting with the right suppliers?
4. How do you ensure that the suppliers that contract with you are, and continue to be, sustainable, ethical, profitable and appropriate for your ongoing needs?
5. Do you know what the impact would be if there was a failure in one of your key suppliers (e.g. it goes out of business or is unable to obtain goods)?
6. Are you confident that you know which suppliers are growing, which are stagnating and which are failing?
7. Have you got business continuity plans and contingencies in place in the event of a key supplier failure?
8. How strong are the relationships with your key suppliers?
9. Do you know what risks are inherent in your supply chain?
10. Do you know how resilient your key suppliers are?
11. How successful are your suppliers in dealing with CSR, not just in having a policy but actually living and breathing and engaging with the many facets within this topic?

As outlined in the Introduction, we will look at some topics from multiple viewpoints, encouraging you to consider procurement from the view of senior leadership, procurement professionals, internal customers including contract managers and the ultimate contract beneficiaries. The optimal results will only be achieved by all parts of an organisation working together, and to do this, all stakeholders must understand the importance of their contribution, and how commercial decision making is at the heart of delivery of organisational strategies.

Director/senior manager

As a director or senior manager you should be confident that you are getting value for money from your supply chain and that your suppliers are operating ethically and sustainably with secure systems and processes in place. Depending on your organisation your external expenditure could range from 30 to 70 per cent. As explained elsewhere in this book, the more that is saved from reducing costs and working capital or by improving quality, on-time delivery or reducing lead time the more, better services you can provide to your end-customers; however, as we have seen in the case of Carillion, if you don't know whether a supplier is profitable or not or if you are squeezing its profits to such an extent that it squeaks, then there is going to be a consequence on how it delivers services or, more fatally, if it remains in business or not. You need to have enough information about that supplier's business and its correlation within the marketplace to know the difference between a win-win encounter and a win-lose encounter.

From a risk perspective, as a director or senior manager, you should be interested in any **significant or recurring** supply chain disruption, poor delivery performance, substandard quality, process inefficiency, legal or regulatory noncompliance or outright fraud which may have an adverse impact on your budget, reputation or performance. In particular for your key/important/strategic suppliers, do you know their financial status, how they are performing, what the risks are to you, any added value initiatives or innovation that they are undertaking which could benefit your organisation? Do you get an annual, half yearly or quarterly report on all your key suppliers? If you do, what do you do with it? At the Foreign, Commonwealth & Development Office the Board receives quarterly dashboard reports on all their key suppliers from the nominated Supplier Relationship Management team. In addition, your procurement team should have an up-to-date procurement risk register which the Board reviews on a regular basis.

At the pre-tender and tender stage your involvement in the supply chain is likely to be at the decision-making level such as agreeing the business case or approving the outcome from a tender exercise. It is also important that you support your procurement team to engage with suppliers, perhaps through supplier days or market testing exercises. Although there is widespread concern among public sector organisations about the extent to which consultation with the market is permitted under the procurement rules, it is a legitimate means of understanding the suppliers and supply chain. Your role is to ensure that buyers and service managers have the necessary expertise and time to engage appropriately with suppliers.

The impact of poor supplier selection should not be underestimated and it can lead to significant underperformance across your span of responsibility and beyond during the life of the contract. There are many books, models and courses which focus on this subject and your procurement team will be well versed in managing the tendering process including supplier evaluation and selection. Your role is to embed the right culture of innovation and probity and ensure that your procurement team understands your vision and direction of travel so that it can articulate this to the marketplace. Thus, your key suppliers become, almost, an extension of your organisation, aligning with your needs, and they can help to bring innovation into the organisation (see Chapter 7 – 'Think differently' and Chapter 8 – 'Encourage innovation' for more ideas on how to do this).

Procurement professional

Understanding your suppliers and the supply base that supports your organisation is your bread and butter. It's what you are paid for. Whether you are the director or head of procurement with overall accountability for the function, a category or sourcing manager with responsibility for a specific area of spend, or a member of the procurement support team, you will have considerably more knowledge and expertise in managing suppliers and the supply chain than anyone else in your organisation.

There are many tools, techniques, processes and models that you can utilise to help you and make your life easier when managing suppliers and the supply chain at every stage in the procurement process; a list of some of them, including where you can find more information about them, is included in the Appendix Glossary. This is by no means an exhaustive list and no doubt new tools, techniques and the necessary systems to support them will be created as markets and the environment we operate in evolve.

Having the tools and techniques to manage the supply chain is one thing, but having the commercial acumen to deal with the complexities relating to the supply marketplace is quite another. A key element of this is understanding the mindset of corporate suppliers to obtain the best commercial, sustainable, corporate and political outcomes for the organisation. This includes understanding the commercial motives and drivers of the suppliers and being able to take calculated risks in implementing efficient sourcing projects to deliver innovative solutions. This is often the most difficult area for public sector purchasers to second guess. Find out what's in it for your suppliers. Having good commercial acumen means being able to weigh up data from various sources and present procurement options and solutions after having engaged with a range of suppliers, experts or researchers. Don't just consult with existing suppliers: after all, if that is all you do, you will likely only get what you have always got.

We find that much of the focus in client organisations is on cost or efficiency rather than understanding the risk and resilience within the supply chain. Following the COVID-19 pandemic we are more likely to see organisations developing much more focus on risk and resilience to minimise the impact of future disruptions. We must, however, be wary of 'fighting the last war' rather than preparing for the next one. Resilience isn't just about reserves or stockpiles, it is also about agility, predictive and prudent planning, awareness and sensitivity to change. Supply chain resilience is about being prepared so that when the risk or disruption to the supply chain happens the organisation knows what to do – this can be switching to alternative suppliers or communicating with customer services teams to change delivery processes or mitigate risks. It's about knowing what you will do if your supplier is found to be breaking legislation, using forced labour (modern slavery), polluting the environment or something similar. Your role is to work with the Contract Manager and supplier to ensure that there is a plan in place for all key suppliers and that there is an up-to-date procurement risk register which is reviewed at Board level. This will include regular financial reviews of suppliers using tools such as Plimsoll, Experian or Dun & Bradstreet (D&B) reports. Often these will be the first indication that there may be something amiss with a supplier; its risk rating may increase and you may need to put your mitigating strategy into practice. Make sure that you get trained in how to interpret the various tools – this is your role and not that of accountants!

Contract/service/delivery manager

As the contract or service manager you will often have an in-depth knowledge about the suppliers that you deal with. You will often be the main contact with the supplier on a day-to-day basis and therefore be in an ideal position to gauge if things are going wrong or, indeed, if there are potential changes with the supplier (new boss or personnel, new acquisition, quality, delivery or upstream supply chain issues, etc.) that may impact your organisation. You should have a close working relationship with the procurement department and you should meet regularly to discuss how the supplier is performing. These sessions are also good opportunities to ensure that you understand any financial updates about the supplier that the procurement team has collated.

Understanding your suppliers and the supply chain is fundamental in being able to make the most of their potential strategic contribution to your organisation. You can assist in this at all stages in the procurement process including participation in the pre-market engagement, development of the specification and KPIs, evaluation of suppliers during the tender phase and during the contract delivery phase.

What would that result in for the end-customer?

In some organisations, such as housing associations, local authorities or the education sector it can often be the end-customer who benefits the most from the effectiveness of your supply chain. She or he can also be the first to spot when things are not going well and, boy, will she or he tell you promptly if a supplier is delivering a service which is less than they expected, often taking to social media to complain about the problem. Conversely, suppliers will often also be closer to the end-customer than you are, so take the opportunity to quiz them about what they see the end-users wanting. Their insights into what end-users need from the service could help focus your discussions on the outcomes rather than the outputs; however, assuming that you are effectively managing the supply chain from a commercial perspective this will have a positive impact on your customer base. Even when things go wrong, as they inevitably will, you and your suppliers should have the necessary processes and people in place to mitigate or negate the issue. A happy customer is the nirvana. Providing the right solutions that make them happy with limited resources is your mission.

Chapter 5 | Know the Markets – ROAD© Part 2

'This above all: to thine own self be true, And it must follow, as the night the day, Thou canst not then be false to any man.'

Polonius in William Shakespeare's (1564–1616)
play 'Hamlet', Act 1 Scene 3

William Shakespeare's advice about getting your own house in order first, before facing the world at large, may have had a more sinister backdrop but, to some extent, it sums up the two-stage approach of getting the most out of your procurement. In Chapter 3 – 'Know what is really needed' we considered the benefits of investing upfront, to look internally and develop a clear understanding of what it is you want to buy. In this chapter, we turn our attention externally, looking at how increasing our understanding of the markets we are buying from can increase the chances of a successful procurement.

This second, external-facing stage, of the ROAD© process is known as the '**Observe**' phase. Observing the market is key to the overall process. If intelligence is the ability to think, to learn from experience, to solve problems, and to adapt to new situations, then it is just as important to be an intelligent customer and, at these levels, it is crucial to be an intelligent procurer. To be an intelligent procurer we need to get to know the potential bidders, suppliers, producers, and their business environments.

To do this, you need to be able to answer several key questions.

Using the outputs from the Research phase, we can start with the obvious question: Who could successfully provide this for me? Whilst it will depend on a few factors including the knowledge gained during the Research phase, an initial list developed during a simple brainstorming exercise can often be sufficient to identify organisations who could potentially supply the goods or service that you are looking to buy.

There is a need to be pragmatic here. Whilst the more comprehensive the list from this initial research is the better, there will be a law of diminishing returns here. The list just needs to be 'good enough' to give you the confidence to know that, as you investigate and engage with the market further during the 'Observe' stage, the responses you get and the conclusion you draw from them are representative of the organisations and market(s) that will eventually participate in procurement. You are not inviting them to tender at this stage, merely understand the market.

A by-product of this initial exercise is that you will have started to answer the second key question: How big is the potential supplier base? The aim here is to push your knowledge further, going from a simple list of potential providers to a better understanding of their size, their presence in different sectors and their experience of delivering against the Operational Statement of Requirement (OSR) developed in the Research phase.

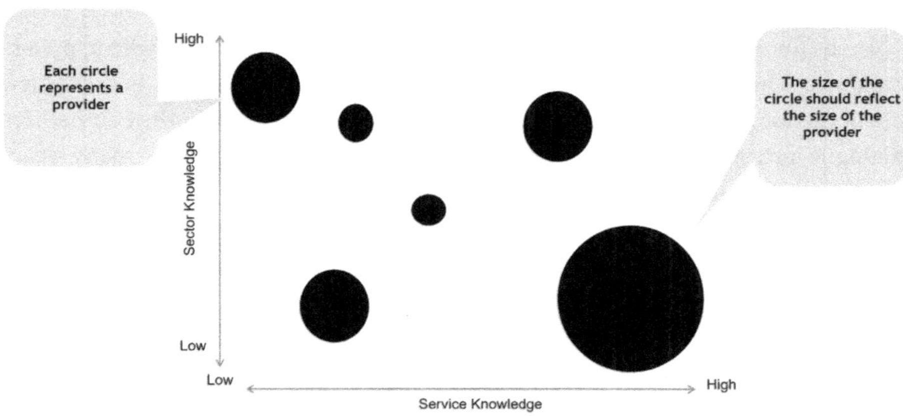

Figure 5.1. Initial analysis of supplier base.

In some organisations, the existing internal knowledge of the market may be sufficient to answer this question. In others, they may wish to engage external support from associations or specialist advisers to ensure this work can be completed quickly and effectively, so that the emerging picture accurately reflects the current situation.

Pre-procurement engagement with the market

Whilst you should now be confident that you have a good picture of the potential supplier base and its capability and capacity, up to this stage you have relied on your own knowledge or the knowledge of your advisers. This is essentially you looking out into the marketplace and forming your views and opinions on its current state and what might happen when you take your requirement to market. It is also important, however, to put yourself in the shoes of the supplier, seeking to look from its perspective and understand what will impact its response to your requirements when they are published. This will ultimately drive the value proposition. This can be done through pre-procurement market testing and engagement.

Fact: It is not against procurement law to talk to potential suppliers before starting a formal procurement process.

Pre-procurement engagement with the market (including talking to potential suppliers) was not prohibited by EU procurement law and it is not anticipated that it will be prohibited by any UK legislation in the near future. Nor is it subject to any detailed procedures, although it must not prevent an effective competition taking place once the formal procurement has started.

In the public sector, however, there is often a reluctance to engage with suppliers once it is known that a procurement is likely to take place. This is not a new phenomenon; the UK government identified an over-reliance on the competitive dialogue process at the expense of pre-procurement engagement many years ago.[10] Since then, it has introduced a number of measures designed to speed up the procurement process and improve the outcomes from it by encouraging appropriate engagement with the market to help shape and refine requirements before the formal procurement starts.

Both the contracting authority and potential suppliers can benefit in multiple ways from early two-way communication. Well-designed and effectively delivered pre-procurement market testing and engagement can help you to:

1. Manage the market – by stimulating increased interest and, therefore, competition. This can be particularly useful if you are looking to reduce the dependency on a limited number of suppliers.
2. Refine the requirements – by improving your understanding of the market's ability to deliver them, what drives costs for potential providers and the other key factors that will impact their value proposition positively or negatively. It is much more difficult to change your requirements once the formal procurement process has started without potentially falling foul of the law.

---

10. Procurement Policy Note. (2012) *Procurement Supporting Growth: Supporting Material for Departments*. Available at: https://www.gov.uk/government/publications/procurement-policy-note-04-12-procurement-supporting-growth-supporting-material-for-departments

3. Gain a better understanding of the feasibility of your requirement – the best approach, the capacity of the market to deliver it, and the possible risks involved.
4. Reduce procurement timescales – by minimising the dialogue needed during the formal procurement process. This will help to complete all but the most complex procurements within 120 working days (from advertising to award).
5. Minimise the need to use complex and costly routes to market such as competitive dialogue.
6. Encourage a more responsive market – by making sure the market is expecting your requirement and has sufficient time to prepare to meet demand, for example by ensuring the right skills and resources are in place.
7. Provide the market with an opportunity to ask questions, raise queries and flush out and resolve any potential issues at an early stage.

There are, however, some important 'do*s* and don't*s*' to remember when conducting a pre-procurement engagement exercise.

It is important to engage early and widely with the market, to give potential suppliers an opportunity to shape the requirement and get ready to meet the demand. Generally, the earlier and the wider the engagement, the better but, as always, there is a need to be pragmatic here to ensure the return on investment in these early stages is optimised.

You need to make sure you are speaking to an appropriately proportionate number of potential suppliers in relation to the market size. You also need to ensure that the outcomes you agreed in the Research stage are shared with these suppliers, so they have the same context as you when you are discussing the Operational Statement of Requirements with them. Critically, you must make sure that all the suppliers involved in any pre-procurement engagement are fully aware that any resulting procurement will be conducted competitively.

It is important to consider in advance how you will maintain the commercial confidentiality of any information received during discussions with potential suppliers, to ensure both you and the suppliers' understanding of how laws, such as the Freedom of Information Act 2000, apply to this data and information.

During any pre-procurement engagement you should discuss whether splitting a contract into smaller contracts or lots would stimulate greater competition and deliver better value for money and encourage participation by more small-to-medium-sized enterprises (SMEs) who can introduce more innovative solutions (so long as it doesn't look like an attempt to circumvent above-threshold procurements), or whether this can be achieved through encouraging a more diverse supply chain. You should also discuss with the market how the requirements might be made more exportable overseas – for example, by using internationally recognised product standards.

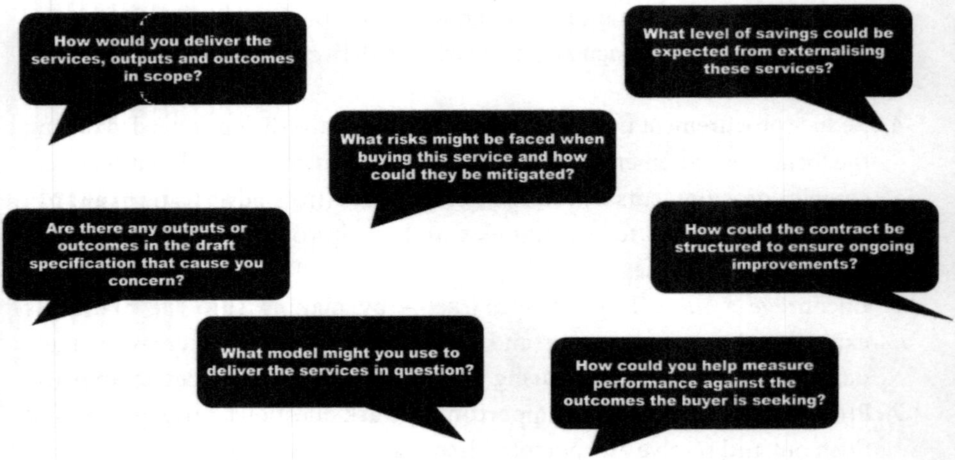

Figure 5.2. Possible questions for a market testing exercise.

Whilst not subject to a formal set of procedures like the procurement process itself, there are several things you must not do during this early market testing and engagement activity because they could jeopardise both the outcomes and the legality of the subsequent procurement. For example, you must not give any one potential supplier an advantage over another when it comes to bidding. This might, for example, occur if one supplier was provided with substantially more information than another and can be overcome by publishing all the information on your website to ensure equal access.

You must also ensure that you do not engage in a way that disadvantages any potential supplier or group of potential suppliers – for example, SMEs and mutuals – and that, following any pre-procurement dialogue, you do not shape your requirement in favour of one potential supplier.

Market testing (using suppliers to shape requirements) and market engagement (helping potential suppliers to work with the contracting authority) can be undertaken in many ways. Some of the more common approaches are listed below.

Market sounding exercises might include the use of questionnaires or crowd-sourcing (obtaining information or input by enlisting the services of a large number of people, typically via the internet). They can be useful in establishing the feasibility, capability, maturity and capacity of the market as a whole.

Product surgeries can be used where a contracting authority has an idea of what they want to buy, and provide an opportunity to allow potential suppliers to present possible solutions

Prior Information Notices (PINs) can be issued to inform the market of your upcoming procurement need and your desire to seek feedback from potential suppliers.[11] Contract Notices or Expressions of Interest for lower value contracts can also be issued on Contracts Finder and can be published in trade journals in order to stimulate market engagement and allow a contracting authority to assess levels of interest.

Supplier days or industry days, sometimes referred to as 'boot camps', can be used to capture potential suppliers' views on your requirements, including viability and possible delivery options. This has the potential to stimulate innovative solutions from a diverse range of potential suppliers. They also provide an opportunity for potential suppliers to discuss opportunities with one another, providing the opportunity for partnering arrangements, potential consortia, or sub-contracting arrangements to emerge.

One final question that should be answered at this stage is how strong your organisation's negotiating position will be when it gets to the procurement stage. A useful tool to assist in the assessment of this is Porter's 5 Forces[12] (hence the cartoon at the start of this Chapter) which helps you to analyse whether a market is **'attractive'** (organisations competing in it are more likely to make a profit) or **'unattractive'** (organisations are less likely to make a profit) to the providers bidding to deliver the service in question. The Five Forces are: threat of **new entrants**; threat of **substitutes**; bargaining power of **customers**; bargaining power of **providers**; and **industry rivalry.**

Bargaining power of **customers** (the purchasing organisation) and bargaining power of **providers** (the supplier organisations) are the two forces of most interest when carrying out a procurement exercise.

Some environments will find the Observe stage more important than others and some will find it easier to conduct than others. The key thing here is to stay focused on the overall intent – to improve the potential for any subsequent procurement to be completed expediently and successfully, delivering the 'Six Rights', addressed in Chapter 3 – 'Know what is really needed'. The most important thing to remember is that the approach and activities set out in these two chapters are intended to be doctrine not dogma. They are specifically designed to be flexed and scaled, and should be adapted to your specific circumstances. The goal should always be to obtain the highest possible return on this upfront investment of effort in terms of the speed, cost and eventual outcomes of the subsequent procurement. Whilst

11. The use of PINs must be in accordance with Regulation 11 of the Public Contracts Regulations and Regulation 14 of the Defence and Security Public Contracts Regulations 2011.
12. Porter, M. (1979) *How Competitive Forces Shape Strategy*, Harvard Business Review. Available at: https://hbr.org/1979/03/how-competitive-forces-shape-strategy

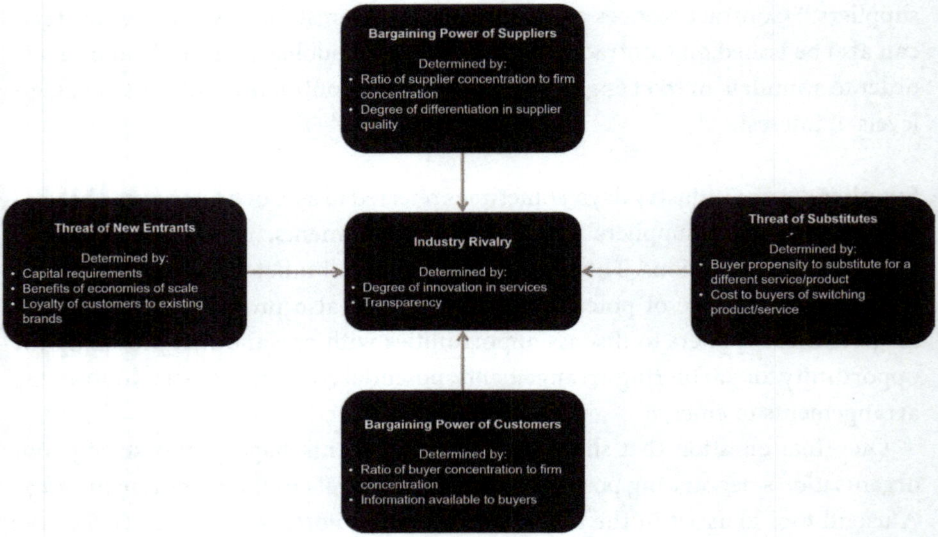

Figure 5.3. Porter's 5 forces.

not always necessary, if used appropriately the input and expertise of specialist external advisers can certainly help when it comes to getting this balance right.

Bringing it all together

Once you're confident that you understand what you want to buy and what the market can offer, the next stage is to *'Orient'* your initial OSR, against what you have learnt from the market.

Completing the diagram below can be a useful orientation exercise, to clarify the areas of alignment and tension in the initial OSR.

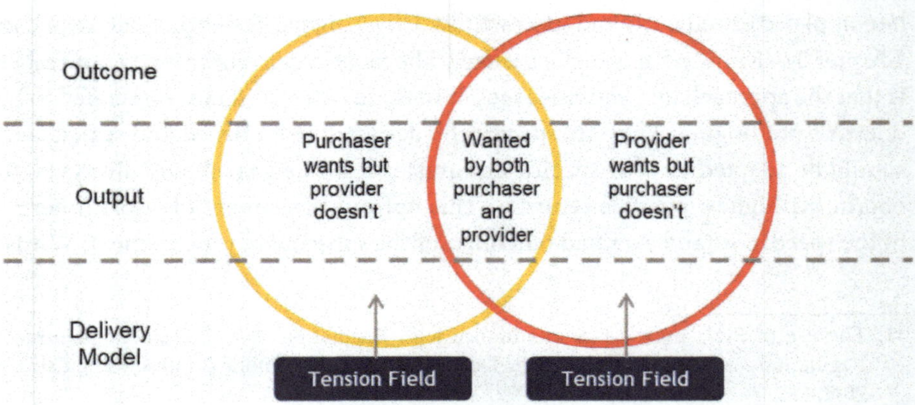

Figure 5.4. Orientating your requirement to the market.

As part of the 'Orient' stage, an options assessment framework can also be used to compare and contrast how different delivery models, for example, which of in-house, outsourced or a blended model, would best meet your key criteria in the light of what you have heard from the market.

Orientation naturally leads on to the need to *'Adjust'* the outline specification to what is achievable by the market and affordable for the contracting authority. Achievability also takes the time factor into consideration. Returning to the helicopter example, an organisation might strongly believe an invisible helicopter is the best way to meet its requirement: however, if one does not exist, this will not be a possibility. There may be no suppliers researching invisibility at present, but one is planning to do so. If the required timescale is long, then this factor may be achievable and there is no need to adjust the specification. If, however, the Orientation stage illuminates a severe mismatch between the requirement and what is achievable, then the specification must be re-aligned before the procurement process can continue.

Failure to adjust the OSR when a requirement to amend it has been identified during orientation is likely to waste time later in the procurement process as suppliers either struggle to devise methods to partly achieve specification or decide not to bid from the outset. A realistic specification invites a better tender process.

Having oriented and adjusted your requirements, you are now in a position to 'Define' and document a final set of requirements and your preferred route to market. It is also important to think about contract management, even during pre-procurement and, if possible, you should be seeking to define and document the core performance metrics for the future contract at this stage. Good quality metrics make contract management easier. Making sure any proposed metrics are SMART[13] is a helpful tool. It is also never too early to think about how and when you might need to end or renegotiate any contract.

13. Doran, G., Miller, A., and Cunningham, J. (1981) *There's an S.M.A.R.T. way to write management goals and objectives.*

SMART metrics are: Specific, Measurable, Attainable, Realistic and Timely. An example of a SMART metric would be:

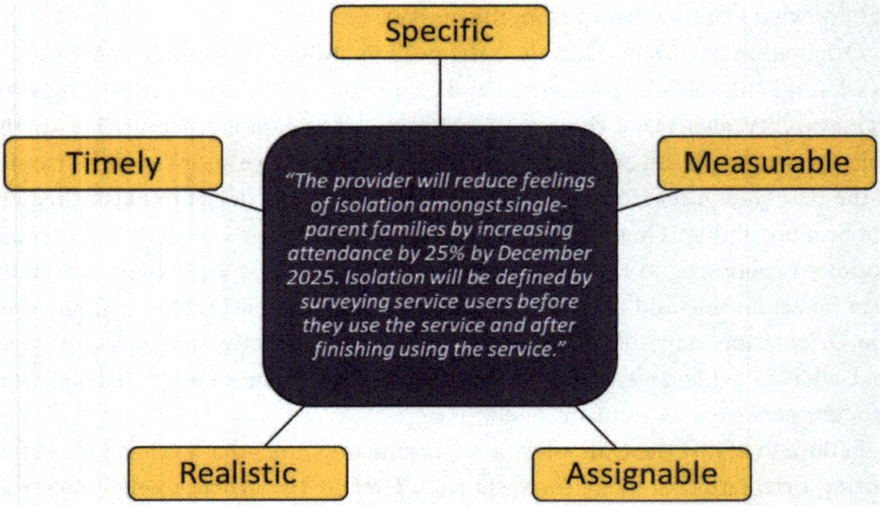

Figure 5.5. Smart metrics – an example.

At this stage, we should also be sufficiently informed to define and document the key risks associated with the procurement we are proposing. These may be risks arising from the specification, the route to market or the market itself, but it is important to ensure that they are identified and assessed as well as ensuring that decisions are properly documented on how they will be monitored, mitigated and managed throughout the procurement process.

Finally, you should define and document the relative importance of quality, price, sustainability and social value to your procurement and define how you will evaluate the different aspects of any bids in relation to one another.

Having completed this process, you will now have all the information you need for your organisation to *'Decide'* on what action to take to seek approval for your proposals. Whilst it is never possible to guarantee the decision makers in your organisation will give you the outcome you want, following this approach will guarantee that you have had the opportunity to provide them with all the context and background information needed to make an informed, evidence-led decision.

Chapter 6 | Be Aware of the World Around You

'Awareness without action is worthless.'
Phil McGraw, American clinical psychologist

Awareness is defined as '*the knowledge or perception of a situation and/or fact*' by the Oxford Languages website.[14] Building on that basis is the concept used within many organisations today, of 'commercial awareness'. This refers to a clear understanding of the daily happenings or developments within an organisation and the wider environment in which they operate. The ability to recognise the importance of this is fundamental to the success of any organisation.

Learning from that approach it is important that those making business decisions have an in-depth knowledge and understanding of the following factors. Can you, as a member of an organisation, confidently answer the following:

1. How does the sector you work in currently operate? What does the future look like?
2. What are the challenges faced by your sector? Can you explain the short and long-term solutions to these challenges?
3. Can you explain the current demographic trends and service demands?
4. What are the political, economic, and social factors impacting your organisation, at a local and global level? What are your responses?
5. How is the wider sector behaving? How does this impact you?

If you are unable to answer any of the above, it is likely you would struggle to meet your service users' needs successfully, limiting your opportunity for success!

---

14. *Oxford Languages*. (2021). Available at: https://languages.oup.com/

For any organisation, opportunities are never in short supply. However, what separates those that take advantage of these opportunities from those that do not, is their understanding of awareness. Those more attentive to the world around them can prepare, plan, and respond effectively. For example, within a business, you would **prepare** by examining the political, economic, and social trends within your industry, on a local and global scale. You would **plan** by analysing the potential impacts these trends have on your organisation, and you would **respond** by introducing short and long-term solutions to secure the longevity of your business.

The concept itself may sound like common sense, '*be aware of the world around you*'; however (and I will keep repeating the point), your knowledge and recognition of it can be fundamental to the success or failure of your organisation. Let us take a very real-life example – the COVID-19 pandemic – because it is one we can all relate to. It has been one of the biggest global challenges impacting billions, both professionally and personally. Any organisation that did not engage early to protect its business following government guidelines would have been negatively impacted. Some examples of businesses changing their strategy to respond to the COVID-19 pandemic were: restaurants switching to offer a takeaway option; workout classes moving online; small businesses setting up websites thereby increasing their online presence and utilising social media. These are very simple examples but demonstrate that those businesses recognised the need to change. As their environment changed, they have now been presented with many opportunities. They have diversified and expanded their business portfolios – something they may not have even considered before. They have also increased their customer base which, in turn, will positively impact the longevity, success, and efficiency of their business. This highlights the positive correlation between business growth (if defined as sales) and awareness.

Director/senior manager

So far, I have reinforced the importance of awareness of the world around us; however, just knowing the concept and not applying it would be pointless.

It is the responsibility of the senior leadership within any organisation to instil the significance of this concept in their employees. The key is to make it part of the organisation's DNA so, by doing this, staff become (sub-)consciously aware of its importance. In addition, it is key for senior staff to drive continuous learning and knowledge, so it is ingrained in the day-to-day thought process of their employees.

For this to be instilled, senior management should develop a strategy incorporating awareness.

Senior leaders who regard strategic awareness as important understand that their sector is always changing and can be unpredictable. This means they do not settle and may utilise opportunities that others, who are not strategically aware, would not have recognised. If, as a leader, your thinking is too one-dimensional (a one-size-fits-all approach) your capability to react to beneficial information is quashed. It also begs the question whether your organisation is agile enough to succeed in a world that is continuously evolving. If you do not make yourselves aware of these changes and keep up, you will simply be left behind to the cost of your service's customers!

Strategy and awareness go hand in hand, and both are needed to be able to deliver long-lasting results; however, it is important to note that both work very differently. If you have awareness *without* strategy it can result in senior leaders fixating on their own ability and generating too many ideas, effectively quantity over quality. In essence, the ideas incorporate awareness, which is great; however, as no clear solution has been considered to bring the ideas to fruition, the effort is rather futile. 'Management by initiative' (often spectacular that benefit the originator's profile rather than the end-customer) without a strategy to deliver on those initiatives will divert staff inappropriately from their core missions and eventually lead to 'initiative fatigue'.

Conversely, strategy *without* awareness means harnessing a one-dimensional thinking. Senior leaders can become so focused on developing a strategy that they lose sight of the changes happening in their wider environment, rendering that strategy ineffective and unrealistic. They may also overlook innovation as the fixed strategy is deemed the correct and only way to succeed.

It is essential for senior leaders to drive and instil (strategic) awareness throughout their organisation. This can be achieved by:

1. Offering and organising learning opportunities.
2. Regular testing of staff to ensure effective learning.
3. (If budget allows) installing a dedicated team whose sole responsibility is to be aware of the local/global market trends/behaviours.
4. Encouraging staff to challenge the status quo and to ask questions about what's happening in the world around them.
5. Ensuring an environment is created in which staff feel comfortable to challenge and, if something is not turning out as you predicted, understanding why and what you need to do to correct that.
6. Developing an organisational strategy that has the correct level of buy in.
7. Encouraging staff to be aware of any changes, particularly anomalies.
8. Being switched on to what is happening in related industries and sectors.
9. Identifying challenges early on within your organisation.
10. Taking risks and ensuring you manage them incredibly well.
11. Seizing opportunities.

12. Using open-minded analysis of your market research without preconceived judgments.
13. Being aware of unique and interesting market trends and understanding how they relate to you, if at all.
14. Never settling!

Any strategy that is put in place must take into consideration the current economic situation; this is what brings the thinking 'into the real world'. For example, let us consider a private sector scenario in which there are high levels of unemployment, reductions in consumer income and high levels of uncertainty. In this situation, consumer spending habits change massively, due to a reduction in consumer disposable income and the high levels of uncertainty, leading consumers to become more risk averse. If a business turned a blind eye to this and continued as normal, it would see its business negatively impacted, through reduced growth or sales, for example. Therefore, the business must adapt to take these factors into consideration, whether that be changing the costing model to reduce upfront costs, so the prices reduce for the customer; increasing its brand awareness to harness the loyal customers; seeking other markets; or utilising other channels, such as social media, to promote its products. Whatever it is, it must be enough to change the mindset of the consumer. The ability to adapt tactics in response to the unpredictability of the market will highlight how robust a business is. This principle is no less relevant to the public sector.

Procurement professional

Just as it is important for senior leaders to highlight and drive the importance for strategic awareness, it is key for a procurement professional to keep that drumbeat going and to implement the directives that are put in place. While the directors may say a strategy is required, procurement professionals would be responsible for utilising their knowledge and experience in the market with suppliers and stakeholders (internal and external) to formulate and draft the strategy for the organisation so that it is relevant and topical. If senior leaders do not communicate a clear strategy to you, consider asking them about aspects highlighted in the paragraphs above to either motivate them to find the answers, ask you to provide them, or share an extant strategy that they simply haven't published anywhere. It shows you care, are aware, and have the best interests of your organisation at heart.

Staying relevant and 'up-to-date' with what is happening in the world is also key for you individually. As previously discussed, this sort of knowledge could change and impact the decisions made later. Within procurement, the key concept that is at the centre of everything is: 'Is it value for money?' Active awareness will help answer that, so constantly ask yourself questions, put yourself in the shoes of the Chief Executive and ask: 'What would I do?' Create hypothetical scenarios and understand how you would react and respond to those situations.

Supplier relationship management is as important within procurement as cost savings are. Utilise the relationships you have to gain inside knowledge of that sector and market. Understand how both are responding and how that will impact you. Is there anything further you need to put in place because of this information? Utilise the strengths and relationships you have built! These can then be used to inform any commercial decisions made. For example, you may highlight that it is sensible to investigate an up-and-coming market or supplier and get preferential rates as it is emerging. Conversely, you may look to hold shorter contracts if you feel the market is not looking as appealing. This may prevent you from dealing with any claims from suppliers, prompted by market changes – especially if they end up costing you more in money and time to resolve than the contract is worth. You want to ensure you are protecting taxpayers' money and spending it effectively and efficiently so you get best value for money.

Contract/service manager

Another element that is just as important as having a strategy in place, is to ensure you monitor the success of it, whether that be through regular KPI reviews or analysis of the impacts that awareness has had on decisions. This allows senior leaders to highlight the areas that require more focus so that solutions can be put in place. If this does not happen, you have no way of tracking success and highlighting areas for improvement. Reviews such as this will ensure productivity is maximised and drive efficiencies within the business. I find it important to reach out and ask for feedback so that I am continually improving, or to find a system or solution that is the most effective for my organisation.

It is important to note that if you are a Contract Manager you should be very switched on when it comes to awareness. This can be in terms of changes in legal obligations, both locally and globally, understanding suppliers within your industry so you can appreciate what good looks like, utilising lessons learnt to your advantage, having relevant up-to-date specialist knowledge and continuing to maintain this to ensure contracts are being performed as they should. This allows for processes to be put in place to limit the level of disruption. It also allows you to manage and view the contract more holistically and adapt quickly to change using your professional expertise to the full.

If you are part of the finance team you would be able to provide the organisation revenue data alongside any strategies in place. Your procurement colleagues will then be able to look at both through spend analysis to analyse the impact that awareness has on outcomes. There is an imperative for public sector organisations to focus on service improvement: How can we do this better? If you have the numbers in front of you, it will highlight clearly how important awareness is and why it should always be incorporated into organisational decisions.

On an individual basis, some internal customers may take the initiative to read journals, blogs and reports to widen their knowledge of the world around them. This sort of behaviour should be recognised and congratulated to encourage other employees to follow suit.

What would that result in for the **end-customer?**

As discussed, being more aware of the world around you gives you the opportunity to prepare, plan and respond better to changes in your environment. This means you stay up-to-date with market trends and use them to your advantage, for example by being able to maximise value for money in times of change. There is scope to invest and drive efficiencies, which can ultimately result in an improved service for the end-customer. For example, if you learn that one of your suppliers was about to fold from market analysis and internal conversations, you could respond early by either purchasing a larger quantity of stock (providing delivery is guaranteed) or by finding an alternative supplier. This means that if or when the company does go bust there is not an immediate impact on you financially or immediate loss of service. If, however, you were not aware of what your suppliers were doing, you could easily continue to operate as normal until it is too late and you can no longer provide a service. This could, in turn, increase your costs, constrain your cash flow and limit your ability to reinvest in long-term efficiencies.

'Being aware of your weaknesses could be your biggest strength.'
Gordon Hester[15]

In conclusion, I think it is fair to say that, no matter what your role is within an organisation, the more you tap into your ability to recognise and implement awareness of the world around you, the more success you will bring to your organisation. This awareness can then have other positive knock-on effects to service-users and your community. There is no negative argument about being *aware of the world around you*, so start today and see the success it brings you!

---

15. Abrahamsen, K. (2021) *Strong leaders lean into their weaknesses*, Dentistry IQ. Available at: https://www.dentistryiq.com/front-office/article/14203300/the-strongest-leaders-lean-in-to-their-weaknesses

Part 2 | Think Ahead

Chapter 7 | Think Differently

'Creativity is thinking up new things. Innovation is doing new things.'[16]

Theodore Levitt Economist, HBR Editor

Everyone buys 'stuff' and, not only that, most of us do it almost subconsciously on a daily basis in shops and restaurants; not everyone does it as a professional calling, though. Good procurement professionals use their specialist knowledge and experience to build a platform from which they can buy creatively, producing better value and effect, by thinking differently and knowing when doing the same thing will not continue to get the best result.

In this chapter we will look at some of the activities that can be used to encourage 'different' or creative thinking. Some activities may seem bizarre to some, while other people may initially find them uncomfortable or will actively resist participating, but if they can be persuaded to join in, they will understand what it is to think differently at the end.

Innovation (in its various guises) is covered in much more detail in Chapter 8 – 'Encourage innovation'; however, it is important to understand that to think differently you need to have the will and the ability to innovate. Without this, it will be very difficult to get procurement outcomes that exceed those achieved before. The old adage 'Do what you have always done, get what you have always got' is annoying but relevant for this chapter.

What can be defined as innovation in pre-procurement or, in fact, an innovative outcome post-award will depend upon how the concept is interpreted and valued by supplier, buyer and end-customer. Whilst that interpretation and valuation will again be variable, the final part of this chapter will look at innovation in more detail as a driver to getting procuring organisations and the customers they serve to think creatively.

---

16. Levitt, T. (2002) *Creativity is Not Enough*, Harvard Business Review. This article emphasises the importance of building an organisational culture which is conducive to purposeful action rather than simply abstract idea generation.

A crucial point which will be unashamedly repeated throughout this chapter is that within the public sector, creativity and innovative thinking are not unconstrained. This is public money and there are rules and regulations which must be adhered to regarding how it is spent. The trick is to act differently but work within the boundaries of the regulations to achieve new outcomes whilst remaining legal.

Plymouth City Council (PCC) has created an alliance to improve the lives of people with complex needs by supporting the whole person to meet their aspirations. PCC awarded a multi-million-pound contract to an alliance of local charities to provide services to people with complex needs (homelessness, drug or alcohol misuse, mental illness and offending). The contract is a new way of bringing together commissioners and services in a partnership where power and responsibility are shared collectively for the common good of people with complex needs. The contract, which will run for five years initially with the potential to extend to ten years, enables the Council and other commissioners to build long-term sustainable relationships with local charities and other service providers to plan for the future.

How do you think differently?

There are many books on this subject such as Rod Judkins' *The Art of Creative Thinking* and Matthew Syed's *Black Box Thinking*, and some of these ideas have been drawn from a number of them and have also been implemented successfully into organisations including procurement teams:

Walk a mile in their shoes. Approach the activity as if you were the internal customer, the end-user, the supplier or any other key stakeholder. Really get into the role and engage with the task in hand as your new persona. How would that person react? What is important to him or her? What language would the individual use? Another well-trodden technique which might be easier to convince people to engage in is de Bono's *Six Thinking Hats,* which is worth checking out.

Take a different perspective. Go and sit somewhere else, move the entire meeting to a coffee shop or take away all the chairs and make everyone stand or sit on the floor. It is amazing how this can spark different ideas as people are more (or sometimes less) comfortable.

Get visual. On giant sheets of paper or huge whiteboards get doodling. There are some superb books on visual thinking available and it has gained in popularity recently. Draw the specification. Visualise the plan. Free your mind and see what comes up. A classic warm-up exercise to shift into this mode of thinking is to get everyone to draw the person next to them. It gets everyone laughing and is a great way to break the stigmas related to drawing in public. An example of a rich picture used as part of the ROAD© process is shown in Chapter 3 – 'Know what is really needed – ROAD© Part 1'.

Tell a story. Take some Rory's Story Cubes (or the app) or similar to the meeting and encourage people to describe their plan, specification, approach to market and so on, only using the icons they rolled on the cubes. Clearly this is not going to produce the actual output, but it forces people to think differently as they must describe the task or outcome as a story confined by the dice. Storytelling is as old as the human race and is a great way to communicate creatively. The cubes shown here are the standard set but there are many variants available.

What would my favourite character do? This is at the crazy end of thinking differently but sometimes that is what it takes to jumpstart innovation. Approach the task as your favourite fictional character. How would Lieutenant Columbo run this meeting? Which route to market would Willy Wonka take? What would Yoda think of these KPIs? Told you it was crazy, but you are thinking differently, and that is the point.

These are just the tip of a very creative and exciting iceberg and the internet is awash with many more tools and techniques to switch your train of thought from the usual rails to something much more innovative. As Doc Brown says in *Back To The Future*: 'Roads? Where we're going we don't need roads.'

Let us see how this translates into behaviours and actions across the commercial team.

Director/senior manager

As a director or senior manager, you will have an influence in shaping the wider organisational strategy and business plan in which commercial and, more to the point, innovative purchasing should feature. It has already been mentioned that public sector organisations are expected to achieve more against the backdrop of ever-reducing budgets. Whilst this is not ground-breaking news to anybody, this 'fact' should not be forgotten.

Many of the chapters within this book recommend empowering colleagues to be able to make decisions. When it comes to encouraging colleagues to think differently, the same principle applies. Within your role as a director or senior manager, the gift of empowering colleagues to propose solutions (even if they appear radical or different to accepted normal practice) and to make decisions that are commensurate with their roles is placed firmly in your hands. Empowerment in this case means to delegate appropriate authority with responsibility and give more junior staff a voice – this, in turn, means not only letting them speak and share their ideas, but *listening* to them and, where possible, endorsing or acting on their suggestions.

It is important to remember you have experienced, qualified procurement professionals within your organisation for a reason; allow them the freedom to use their skillset in order to secure provisions that continue to follow in the familiar mantra of 'best value' solutions. They will probably engage suppliers that go the 'extra mile' and offer much more than has been achieved previously – because you have given them the opportunity to be creative. Recognise that creative thinking inevitably involves risk – of both failure and incrementally greater success. Understand and accept these risks, which are discussed further in Chapter 9 – 'Risk is inevitable – embrace it'.

So, what can directors and senior managers do to support their procurement professionals when it comes to providing them the freedom to think differently?

Encourage? No, demand dialogue with suppliers: Without the encouragement of dialogue and 'taking an interest', public sector organisations will continue to obtain the same proposals from suppliers from one contract cycle to the next. No matter how well you may think a supplier has been or is performing, they are not mind readers and need regular engagement to ensure they understand your needs! In addition, by engaging with suppliers the pool of ideas has not just increased, it has also gained a new perspective. Combining these two perspectives could be the key to a new way of thinking and in turn some new outcomes.

Training and development: To reiterate, procurement professionals have to learn continually because the parameters of public buying are continually evolving.

The rate of change has also consistently increased over time. It is important that procurement professionals are given the opportunity to attend training workshops or seminars as well as having access to the latest legislative changes so they can keep abreast of an ever-evolving environment. Leadership should acknowledge that an informed procurement professional will deliver the best outcomes and be armed with the knowledge to inform creative solutions. This is helping understand the lines within which you are working, but don't just restrict this training to procurement skills. There are many books and courses which teach or facilitate creative thinking and it is possible that someone within the organisation already has the skills they can share with their colleagues.

Determine what innovation is trying to achieve: This has to align with the creation and later refinement of the organisational strategy and business plan. Directors and senior managers must create, disseminate and deliver on a vision of what innovation is aiming to deliver on a wider organisation level. If, for example, the driver for innovation is to save money on the bottom line, then the procurement professional must be encouraged and enabled to think differently to implement novel solutions to do so. Conversely, if improved qualitative outputs are required by the organisational strategy or business plan, then the procurement professional must be supported to work with the suppliers and customers (or end-users) to develop suitable specifications, evaluation criteria and so on, to achieve the desired outcome.

Lead by example: The simplest and most effective method for achieving a cultural change within an organisation is for the leaders to adopt that behaviour first. The leadership team should assess their own approaches and consider how often they think differently and what form that difference takes, then ensure this is communicated widely. Thinking differently can be considered risky or even terrifying for some people, so witnessing their leaders taking the first step will help and contribute to those outcomes the organisation is seeking.

Procurement professional

So, the procurement professional has received endorsement and support to think differently from those above them within the organisation – fantastic! It may be a little unconventional to have such freedom of action in terms of how we typically procure provisions. This is especially so given the constraints and parameters set within the Public Contracts Regulations (PCR), and not forgetting our own organisational standing orders, but bear with this train of thought!

To help procurement professionals step beyond simple processing towards a more entrepreneurial mindset, adopting the following principles will help them take the first and subsequent steps into what may be new territory:

Be proactive, not reactive: One of – if not the biggest – challenge for public sector procurement professionals is lack of time, whether it is due to poor planning from the contract manager or end-user or the imperative to spend finance quickly due to a time constraint imposed upon it, for example, in the instance of time-limited grant funding. Develop a forward procurement plan to allow the director or senior manager, the procurement professional and the contract manager or end-customer, alike, to plan and allocate resources appropriately for mid- and longer-term purchases. Once in place, keep it up! Monitoring and revisions will be much more measured and less onerous than continually 'fire-fighting' unexpected requirements. Being on the front foot will allow you to engage in the pre-procurement process, doing the research in the ROAD© process (more detail in Chapter 3 'Know what is really needed – ROAD© Part 1' and Chapter 5 – 'Know the markets – ROAD© Part 2'), and make recommendations to do things in creative new ways.

Build connections: Build a strong relationship with your contract manager and end-users, discussed in further detail in Chapter 2 – 'Be connected'. This may sound obvious but so much of the role of a procurement professional is relationship building, and it is easy to be absorbed in process and the next panic rather than outcomes and people. Having a rapport with them to better understand their needs will supplement the information within the forward plan. It will also provide you with helpful pointers to reshape a purchasing exercise if required, and the ability to think creatively when developing the specification upon which prospective suppliers can base their proposals. A contract manager or end-user, who has a good relationship with the procurement professional, is more likely to inform the incumbent earlier of a new or changing requirement.

Early Supplier Involvement (ESI): Suppliers are very rarely mind readers! Contract managers or end-users will approach procurement professionals with potential and perceived requirements without knowing if a solution can be delivered or, even, whether it is needed. ESI is a concept that has been around in the commercial word for many years and is, most often, aligned to performance, rather than conformance specifications. It is sometimes perceived as free consultancy, before any formal commercial engagement. It can provide insight to market-leading innovative technologies and solutions which could assist the procurement professional to think differently. Some of the advantages that ESI can offer are shown in Table 7.1:

Advantage	Explanation
Quicker development lead time and enhanced quality and lower development costs.	Suppliers get an indication of requirements ahead of formal processes. This means they can mobilise themselves more quickly should they wish to participate.
Improved product specifications and improved manufacturability of products.	Knowledge gleaned from 'free consultancy' means that the 'need' can be met by something that can actually be realised and delivered. Requirements can be better shaped and interpreted by the marketplace when the invitations go out in the form of specifications.
Access to new technologies	Specifications that have been developed with ESI support are likely to be very different to those previously issued on earlier contract opportunities. There should be a reassurance here that what you are asking for within the specification is the latest possible iteration of the provision, but still within the art of the possible.
Shared expertise for problem-solving and exchange of knowledge and information, building trust and alliance	Open dialogue with suppliers through ESI will not only build good relationships but also provide opportunities to share previous experiences. Suppliers will be encouraged to identify and help resolve potential problems with the purchasing organisation's requirement. The supplier relationship could step beyond a purely transactional one towards partnering or even partnership with significant mutual benefits.
Improved understanding of supplier capabilities	This will naturally support the procurement professional when looking to think differently.

Table 7.1. Advantages of ESI.

It is not a competition – share ideas and best practice: Public sector procurement professionals are in a unique position in that 'competition' between peers, in its truest form, is pretty much non-existent. A private sector organisation would not dream of sharing information with a competitor in the same marketspace, but the public sector should not be constrained by such commercial competitiveness. Engage with some different people and be open to their different approaches and thinking.

Look beyond the 'stock' solution: Some may be tempted to simply re-let existing contracts because there have been no complaints about service levels from end-users, or about delivery challenges from suppliers – so check both ends of the supply chain to see if there is a better way of creating the desired outcome. Frameworks appear to be an 'easy' solution because someone else had done the hard work setting them up, but they may not be optimal for your specific needs – again, check. If they are not a perfect fit, consider collaborating with other agencies who have similar needs to provide a bespoke solution. It may be more work initially, but could produce lasting improved outcomes.

Contract manager/end-customer

Contract managers or even end-customers enjoy the unique position that they can identify a requirement and also define it in such a way that it best meets their needs. It is the role of the procurement professional to ensure that these requirements are bought in a compliant, transparent manner. Together, contract managers, end-customers and procurement professionals play a vital role in producing commercial solutions that are better than any provided previously.

Collaboration across this team together with a close working relationship among the contract manager, end-customer and the procurement professional is, therefore, essential to enable a novel or creative procurement outcome. The following are some examples and techniques which can be considered by a contract manager or end-customer when looking to think differently.

Build innovation into specifications: It is important that senior leadership, directors and senior managers are engaged early and encouraged to support innovation when building future specifications. They should understand and endorse the principles that these specifications, enabled by thinking differently:

1. add longer term value to the procuring organisation
2. are in the best interests of all stakeholders
3. drive innovation appropriately to stimulate better outcomes

How contract managers or end-customers achieve this understanding and endorsement for any particular procurement will depend on many variables. These include, but are not limited to, the provision itself, the budget set aside, the marketplace, any contractual term and so on.

> Transport for London (TfL) sought to reduce the whole life-cycle cost of lighting the London Underground network. The procurement calculated external costs including installation, maintenance, energy use, carbon and cleaning costs. Indicative results suggest a 25 per cent saving on whole life-cycle costs, and significant reductions in energy consumption.

Develop creative key performance indicators (KPIs): KPIs are a keystone contract management tool to monitor a contract and supplier performance over its lifetime. A big failing of public sector organisations is that they have historically opted for boilerplate KPIs, regardless of the commercial subject. Managers have then failed to monitor them, resulting in suppliers doing the same and simply 'going through the motions'.

To overcome this nugatory activity and culture, the selection, application and maintenance of KPIs needs to be relevant to the subject matter of the purchase. The most successful follow SMART objectives which are particularly relevant here (See Chapter 5 – 'Know the markets – 'ROAD© Part 2' for more detail):

Specific
Measurable
Assignable
Realistic
Timely

Now that the theory is out of the way, look at how creative KPIs that incentivise suppliers throughout the contract period can be developed. Too many organisations use KPIs as a 'stick' to beat suppliers (that is, when they are monitored) for a 'failure' of a KPI that adds no value or benefit. All KPIs should at least maintain and, preferably, continuously improve value, service and outcomes. A poor service, delivered on time or even early, helps nobody. Neither does an over-performing service delivered late.

Suppliers can be incentivised to continually innovate and still deliver effective outcomes through the use of creative KPIs. This can be helped by the following actions:

1. Build innovation into contract management. Many public sector frameworks run for a period of up to four years; that is a long time in any environment to deliver continually the same provisions against a fixed specification. Encourage and incentivise suppliers to put forward revised and superseding solutions regardless of the maturity of the contract. Benefits of this flexibility include:
   i. the ability to ensure the most up-to-date solutions available
   ii. continuous updating of knowledge about how solutions are evolving ahead of new procurement exercises
   iii. ensuring suppliers are not complacent about providing dated solutions which may become obsolete or do not exploit new technology and processes.
2. Reward added value. This is more than just asking suppliers to 'throw in a few extras at no additional cost'. The issue with a specification, regardless of how much time or research is put into the development, is that a contract manager or end-user can never be 100 per cent sure that it is going to fully meet needs.

i. The suggestion here is that a weighting is applied in the evaluation criteria that identifies 'added value' that may even be beyond core requirements. The 'weight' applied is ultimately the decision of the bid evaluators; examples of limits to 2-5 per cent are common to ensure that focus is maintained on more meaningful elements.
ii. This is an opportunity for the supplier to propose items or deliverables that would further supplement the specification; it is then up to the contract manager or end-user to assess its 'value' and determine an effective return on any perceived investment. For example, how much cheaper would the contract be without the value added (supposing it could be extracted and isn't a 'free good' as an intrinsic part of the solution)?
iii. Any added value can be reflected in a SMART KPI and subsequently monitored over the life of the contract – in turn, adding to future specification development.
iv. Suppliers could be offered a share of the rewards to incentivise them to innovate.

3. Offer contract extensions. Contracts are often broken down so that they consist of an initial term and subsequent extension periods; however, a prospective extension is very rarely seen as a KPI with which to incentivise suppliers. In times of economic uncertainty, commercial organisations seek continuity of supply and, similarly, suppliers need continuity of custom. The offer of a contract extension, subject to satisfactory performance (including continuous improvement) and/or price, can feature as a SMART KPI. If the commercial organisation needs to vary – or prematurely end – the extended requirement, contract break clauses should be incorporated to manage the buyer's options – but, remember, suppliers may look for reciprocal arrangements!

A series of suggestions have been offered throughout this chapter to help build the conditions for thinking differently, but the key driver of creativity is an environment of trust, and empowerment of individuals to free their minds and take calculated risk. This normally has to come from the top, but can happen at any level.

Thinking differently takes effort and imagination. Thinking differently within the constraints of public sector procurement requires a team effort combined with a sound understanding of the dimensions of the box you must innovate within. It can be done, though, and as pressure mounts on commercial and procurement teams to enable their organisations to do more with less it may be the only option remaining for some. Embrace it!

Chapter 8 | Encourage Innovation

'Risk-taking is the essence of innovation.'
Herman Kahn, American futurist

What is innovation?

Innovation is about turning new products and services in your environment into reality. When linked to the commercial process, innovation is about working with suppliers, customers, internal partners, and the market, to generate better ideas before they are developed into tangible products or services.

Innovation does not necessarily mean inventing something never seen before. Taking ideas and best practice from other sectors then adapting them to suit the environment you operate in can also be seen as innovation, albeit with a lower-risk approach from which more creative innovative solutions can be developed. An example of this is the use of automated telephone responses, adopted early by banks to direct customers to appropriate customer service representatives and subsequently expanded in capability over the years. The technology has been adopted by local government which uses it for many requirements reaching from simple call redirection to transactional activity such as paying council tax bills and ordering services and so on. The introduction of Artificial Intelligence into these systems has enabled a truly interactive experience to be adopted.

> *'If you think of standardization as the best that you know today, but which is to be improved tomorrow; you get somewhere.'*
> Henry Ford, founder of Ford Motor Company

Innovation (in public procurement) can deliver a number of benefits such as accelerated technology adoption, support to small and medium-sized enterprises, improved market stimulus and improved performance against the wider procurement objectives.

Innovation can, of course, come in various guises and from multiple sources. This chapter cannot provide a 'catch-all' list of innovative outcomes and benefits, but it would be worth considering the following opportunities and benefits from a procurement organisation perspective:

1. Suppliers that are encouraged to be forward-thinking to generate ideas for continuous improvement throughout the life of a contract and as part of the working relationship itself.
2. Cost savings, profitability and competitive advantage are all possible beneficial outcomes for being the first supplier to bring an innovative product or service to the marketplace. By default, as a procurement organisation working with such suppliers, early adopters are more likely to be provided with market-leading solutions. Similarly, adopting proven solutions from other industries into the public sector provides lower-risk innovation but demands that procurement professionals look outside and beyond their normal horizons.
3. The development of relationships with suppliers may result in more transfer of knowledge and innovation beyond the initial contract or working relationship, putting the buying organisation in a stronger position.
4. Improvements to current products or services could be offered to the buying organisation.
5. The opportunity for procurement to demonstrate the value that it can bring to the wider organisation internally, along with the customers it serves.
6. Supporting the organisation's strategic thought processes regarding the wider encouragement of innovation and knowledge sharing.

Why is it important to encourage innovation?

Nearly every business operates within a market where it faces competition; however, the level of competition within each market varies. Competition, by its very nature, will drive innovation, as suppliers try to win greater market share and become the dominant force. The resulting innovation has huge benefits.

By encouraging innovation, suppliers:

1. improve their products
2. improve their services
3. find new ways of doing things
4. become more efficient
5. employ more cost-effective methods
6. are able to market to a wider audience

How is innovation embedded in the procurement process?

The key areas shown in Figure 8.1 embed innovation into the procurement process and are outlined below.

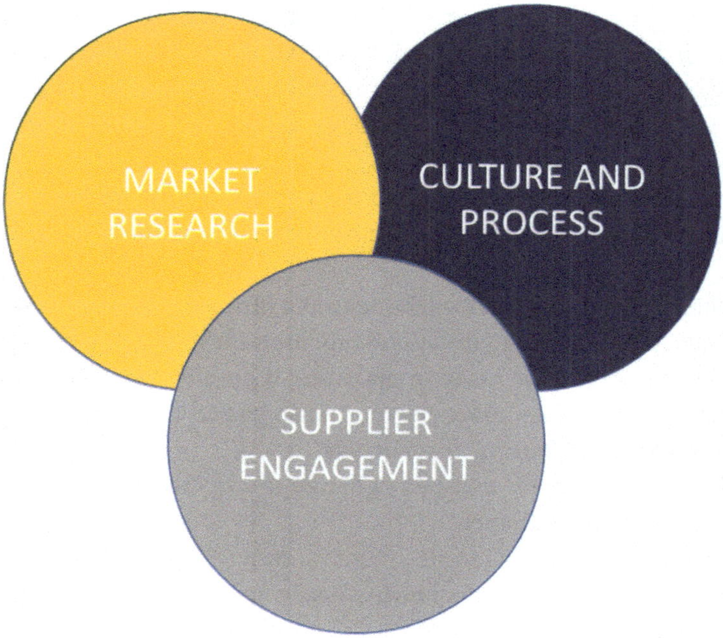

Figure 8.1. Culture and process.

Culture and process

It is imperative that a culture of innovation and continuous improvement is embedded within the procurement process to make the most of the opportunities for better outcomes at every stage including during pre-contract, at contract signing, through-life management and even post-contract activities.

To embed culture, it is necessary to understand the organisation's internal and external processes, who the stakeholders are, their relevant touchpoints, and the purpose of the organisation. The purpose statement or vision must be strong, clear, and inspirational to build belief and responsibility towards achieving a common goal of always striving for better.

Once the factors above are understood, the values and behaviours can be reinforced within these processes which will enable such a culture to thrive. These values must be short, memorable, and unambiguous to have the desired effect. To ensure long-lasting culture change and continued engagement, it is key that those impacted and involved are asked for their opinion and are seen to shape these values and principles. These values and principles must be intrinsically linked to the purpose statement to be embedded successfully.

The greatest opportunity for innovation in procurement is at the beginning of the buying process, prior to a contract being signed when there is no legal constraint on the parties. Once a contract has been signed, the parties are restricted to the terms set out in that contract. Post-contract signature there could still be opportunity to innovate, but this will be limited unless it is specifically included in the terms. This could be your first innovation! Embedding innovation into culture and process could start by looking at opportunities with mobilisation and contract management.

To embed innovation across the end-to-end commercial process, and grow an entrepreneurial culture, it should be considered at the following stages:

1. When determining what will be delivered through the commercial pipeline.
2. When defining the organisation's procurement strategy and what potential approaches could be taken to maximise innovative opportunities in areas such as negotiation, innovation partnerships and commercial partnerships with other procurement departments.
3. When defining a post-contract signature strategy that includes mobilisation and contract management.
4. When defining how you will communicate and engage with your suppliers.
5. When creating SQ/ITT documentation/templates as part of your purchasing exercise.

The possibility of working with a small-to-medium sized enterprise (SME) on an innovative product or service could, eventually, lead to a long-term commercialised partnership. Initially, this product or service may be a pilot, but through collaboration, a new product or service could be brought to market, which could ultimately benefit both parties greatly, for example through royalties. The SME market can be important for bringing more innovative solutions into the public sector but in order to do so the terms and documentation need to allow for flexibility so they can showcase their full ability in other arenas.

Innovation often starts when a 'burning platform' solution is needed. That is, when a novel solution to a problem that is an existential threat is required (another reason why SMEs are often good innovators when they struggle for survival and growth). Building momentum for innovative change to a 'comfortable' status quo is unlikely to happen unless senior leadership can be convinced to initiate it *and* accept the inherent risk in exploring change.

Such a change does not happen overnight but, by embedding the values into operation, those involved will feel a sense of purpose and understanding about how their actions affect the overall culture of the organisation. Communication of these values, both formally and informally, is required to ensure staff retain the values and continue to exhibit the behaviours required.

Market research

Undertaking market research is absolutely key to any successful procurement exercise and plays a big role in innovation. The benefits of this research are wide-ranging and demonstrated in Figure 8.2:

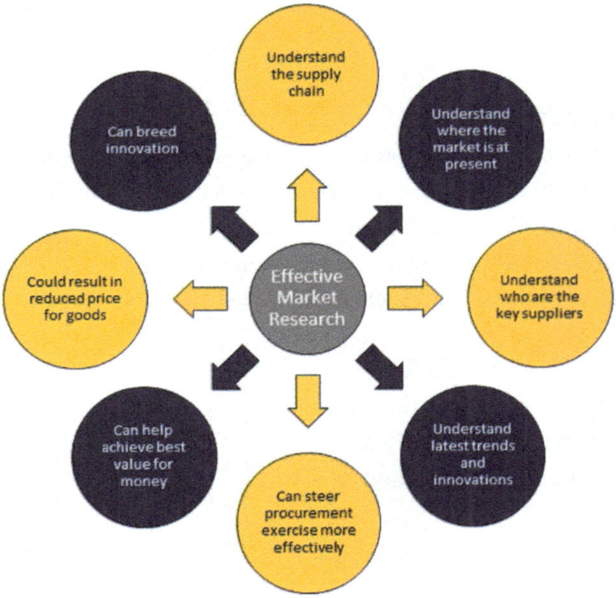

Figure 8.2. The benefits of effective market research.

Market research enables a procurement team to understand the supply chain, where the market is currently positioned, the key suppliers within that market, and the latest trends and innovations. The supply chain is not the only area where innovation can be born, and a procurement team should be conscious of the ability for innovation to come directly or indirectly from customers or other departments within the organisation.

Armed with the information provided by market research, the team can subsequently steer the procurement exercise to achieve best value for money, an improved operation or service, or a reduced price for goods. Thus, market research can be the factor that breeds innovation.

Unfortunately, market research is seen as an administrative burden by some; however, undertaking market research as part of the pre-contractual steps can save time and cost in the long run. The outcome of effective market research is knowledge, which not only assists innovation, but can help with understanding the investment levels required and, in some instances, the indicative timescales required to complete that purchasing exercise.

Not everything needs replacing like-for-like, but how do you know unless you fully understand the existing product's capabilities, the market, and the latest products or services within that market? The answer is you don't, unless you undertake market research. In a rising number of cases, with organisations keen not to spend unless deemed absolutely necessary, changes to business process as a result of market research can provide both short and, in some cases, long-term benefits which eliminate the need to undertake a full procurement exercise.

Supplier engagement

It is imperative that any engagement with the market is done openly, transparently, and fairly, with adherence to the necessary data legislation including the UK General Data Protection Regulation (UK GDPR). It is seen as good practice to research the market beyond when you are required to buy goods and services. Regular research of the key markets that you utilise will improve:

1. knowledge of your market
2. your chances of innovating
3. your time to market
4. the ability to reduce costs and re-work

When dealing directly with suppliers, as part of early engagement it is important that the suppliers are given adequate time to respond to the stated commercial requirement. SMEs with limited resources may require additional time to respond effectively to the requirement and to determine whether they can meet the scope; however, they are generally more agile than large prime contractors. Setting too short a timescale is likely to result in a poor response rate and a poor quality solution. Increased time to engage increases the likelihood of innovation.

Like market research, supplier engagement should be conducted openly, fairly, and transparently. This can be achieved by following correct process, and structuring documentation in a common-sense and jargon-free manner. You should highlight areas in which you wish the suppliers to showcase innovative solutions to meet certain requirements.

'You must have a supplier relationship of constant improvement.'

W. Edwards Deming, widely acknowledged as the leading management thinker in the field of quality

What are the risks of innovation?

Whilst the benefits of innovation are plentiful and well known, including improved productivity, reduced costs, better quality and added value, there are also risks which should be noted. When undertaking an innovative project, such risks should be recognised, mitigated or managed. They can rarely be avoided if true innovation is to happen, and benefits must be balanced against risk – especially when public resource is driving that innovation.

The key risks associated with innovative projects are summarised below:

1. **Continued competition.** Most suppliers are in markets where they face competition. Innovation only leads to a significant competitive advantage if competitors are unable to replicate the innovation relatively easily or quickly.
2. **Uncertain return or outcome.** Innovation is harder to guarantee in terms of output. There is therefore greater chance of failure from an innovation venture, but this has to be weighed against the step-change benefits and returns from successful implementation.
3. **The greater the timescale involved, the greater the risk that the innovation is overtaken by a competitor.** The imperative that drove the innovation may also be solved by another solution, but without the step-change in improved outcomes.
4. **Financial outlay.** Developing new concepts or technology costs money but the rate of return can be higher than projects without innovation at the forefront. The opportunity cost of investing in innovation can therefore be very high. in some instances, no financial return may be achieved.
5. **Misinterpreting the market.** The new product or service could be excellent in terms of meeting the end-customers' needs, but despite these features, the customers may not be willing to pay for it if the costs outweigh the perceived benefits.
6. **Reputational damage.** This is an outcome of the points above, rather than a factor in isolation. A failure to innovate successfully could impact on the organisation, but conversely, failure to innovate could result in stagnation and gradual degradation.

Let us now consider how this translates into how innovation can be encouraged across the organisation:

Director/senior manager

The roles of directors and senior managers in creating an environment where innovation can flourish are laid down in Chapter 7 – 'Think differently'. They include demanding the right behaviours and engagement with suppliers, providing the right tools, training and development and, importantly, placing creativity and innovation upfront in the vision and strategies.

> *'A mind that is stretched by a new experience can never go back to its old dimensions.'*
>
> Oliver Wendell Holmes Jr., Former Associate Justice of the US Supreme Court (1841–1935)

Innovation rarely comes from the top. It is often the result of ideas emerging from non-experts and outsiders 'asking the stupid question' that cannot be answered using current or legacy processes. It may not provide the innovative solutions, but it is part of leadership's role to ask the difficult questions that drive people to think 'outside the box' and then support them by building a culture of innovation. This can be generated internally by making time and giving a 'voice' to a wide section of the community – using workshops, empathy mapping, collaborative play, and other tools.

Creating a culture of innovation which spreads through the entire organisation must be underpinned with strong leadership embracing and promoting innovative change. It may be that a procurement department has to designate individual projects for innovation in order to encourage suppliers to bring forward new ideas. Where applicable, supplier performance could be directly linked to the benefits of any innovation delivered.

Innovation can also be nurtured within the organisation beyond the procurement team – to improve understanding of end-customer needs or to identify solutions with outcomes rather than drive outputs and deliver step-change improvements in performance.

Directors and managers making time and resource available to enable such activity and, more importantly, acknowledging and **implementing** the outcomes from these events, form the first steps in building a culture of innovation. Procurement professionals can be in a good position (between service deliverers, suppliers, and leadership) to drive such events, but must be given the authority to do so.

Procurement professional

> *'Imagination is everything. It is the preview of life's coming attractions.'*
>
> Albert Einstein

Procurement professionals should see themselves as the drivers of innovation. They sit in a privileged position, able to see the end-to-end supply chain from suppliers (and their suppliers) through the organisation's delivery teams to the end-customer. All contracts will normally pass through their hands during their formulation and they are ideally placed to facilitate the sharing of best practice across players in both supply and delivery areas.

The perspective they enjoy when overseeing the creation of higher requirements, standards and outputs as well as individual solutions and products offered should enable them to see gaps that need filling, processes that add little or no value, and areas that are crying out for new thinking. Removed from the unending pressure of delivering results and outcomes at the coal-face of customer service, they should be able to use their professional training, experience and, importantly, imagination to seek if not offer innovative solutions to meet end-customer needs. 'Have we ever thought about doing it this way?' should be part of their mantra.

Contract/service manager

Contract, service and delivery managers are normally closest to the end-customers and should have an intimate knowledge of demands on their suppliers and how they overcome them. They are best placed to feel the emotions generated by outputs and performance at both ends of the support chain. They will be closest to any 'fire' on the 'burning platform' and therefore best motivated to find innovative solutions when they are required.

They should consider their fellow procurement professionals as allies who will help them bring innovative ideas to fruition, not 'blockers' who hide behind process and frustrate their desires to make a difference, or change poor or ineffective practices and solutions. In order to let them help, they must share their ideas early in their genesis, not just when they are fully formed, and keep their minds open to suggested changes that will probably make them more practical realistic and legally compliant! Equally, if their procurement professional comes to them with a novel idea for the future, they should invest their experience in it and not dismiss it out of hand. The 'not invented here' syndrome has stifled great ideas through modern times. Look beyond the initial reasons that something might be impractical to what step-change benefits might be gained if things were done a little differently. What would that result in for the **end-customer?**

Successful innovation might mean significant improvement in service that could transform customers' lives. Equally, it may go unnoticed by customers but reduce the cost of service to them. It should be noted that any innovation involves risk. Some novel ideas may not work, and any impact is likely to be felt by the end-customer.

End-customers should therefore be involved in any innovation, if at all possible, even if it is only seeking their voice on what change is needed, or whether innovative change might be needed or acceptable in the future. If they are invested in the enterprise, they may be more willing to accept sharing or at least understanding some of the risk to outputs and outcomes. If nothing else, they will act as a conscience to ensure that innovation is reasonable, beneficial and needed. A 'Can you suggest a solution?' response to end-customers' queries may then provide you with a game-changing opportunity. If they recognise that there is a culture of creative thinking and innovation in the organisation, they may even be tempted to suggest novel ideas without fear of immediate rejection or worse, ridicule. The 'Why can't you…', 'Why do I have to…' customer questions should be seen as a trigger for innovation, not for putting up defensive walls.

Chapter 9 | Risk is Inevitable – Embrace It

'If you know the enemy and know yourself, you need not fear the result of a hundred battles. If you know yourself but not the enemy, for every victory gained you will also suffer a defeat. If you know neither the enemy nor yourself, you will succumb in every battle.'

Sun Tzu, *The Art of War*

In 2020, did you truly understand what your own operational (business), non-operational and financial risks were? Many organisations had to revisit these areas with increased prioritisation and frequency, ensuring that decision-making was both effective and timely to help mitigate risks that had neither been fully articulated nor explored. Have lessons really been learnt about global supply chains and their reliance on single markets? Well, organisations are beginning to think more broadly, in respect of their supply chains, and those of the contractors they rely upon. Events, during the global COVID-19 pandemic, have demonstrated the fragility of supply chains and an over-reliance on single sources of supply: locally, nationally and across the globe.

It's not just about global events, we also need to think regionally and nationally. It is some time since the 2011 Fukushima earthquake and the subsequent tsunami that halted global automotive production. Professor Carvalho at the Faculty of Economics, in a co-authored book *Supply Chain Disruptions: Evidence from the Great East Japan Earthquake*,[17] suggests that, while an event of this magnitude can directly affect supply chains, there is a broader trickle-down impact across other businesses with the effect that all supply chains suffer, not just the direct few. He states:

'We initially investigated whether the impact we saw could be due to something else, maybe global conditions or poor economic policies that could have been

17. Carvalho, V, M., Nirei, M., Saito, Y, U. and Tahbaz-Salehi, A. (2020) *Supply Chain Disruptions: Evidence from the Great East Japan Earthquake.*

> *enacted at the same time,'* he says. *'However, what we saw was that the quake disrupted supply chains. It shaved off bits of activity throughout the Japanese economy; it wasn't that a few firms got very severely affected, rather it just made every supply chain in Japan less efficient. It affected suppliers and customers of disaster-stricken firms, and then continued cascading through the economy, disrupting firms that had no direct business link to the affected area.'*

Looking back to the Falklands War in 1982 provides a good example of risk management, with both good and bad outcomes. The SS *Atlantic Conveyor* was hit and lost after an attack by the Argentine Air Force on 25 May 1982. The SS *Atlantic Conveyor* was a roll-on roll-off (roro) container cargo ship, carrying essential military equipment, including 25 aircraft, vehicles, tentage and a lot of aircraft bombs. One Chinook, 14 Harriers and one Wessex helicopter were flown off the ship during transit and spread around the fleet to offer an element of protection, but the rest of the cargo was lost. Who, if anyone, took a balanced risk assessment on load composition with key stocks from three separate Services, and what tools did they have to understand that risk? Was it simply a gut decision (sometimes hiding behind the quasi-scientific description of 'military judgement') based on an imperative to 'just do something' when cobbling together a Task Force at incredibly short notice? How much of the risk judgement was shared with the three Services (RN, Army and RAF) who provided the kit for movement and would need to use it at the other end, or was it only undertaken by those responsible for ships' load planning? Was risk management lost in the noise of expediency?

More recently, in 2021 the MS Ever Given had a highly publicised incident in the Suez Canal, blocking it for six days and disrupting global supply chains. The Evergreen shipping line faces a more than £900m bill and many customers faced disruptive delays with their supplies. But could these outcomes have been mitigated?

Nearly 19,000 ships passed through the Suez Canal in 2020 according to the Suez Canal Authority – an average of 51.5 ships per day. The Suez Canal has a good safety record overall with very infrequent shipping incidents. There were 75 reported incidents in total in the canal between 2010 and the end of 2019. More than a third involved container ships (28); however, groundings (such as the Ever Given incident) are the most common cause of shipping incidents in the canal – 25 in the past 10 years or 1 in 3 of all Suez shipping incidents. Insurers have been warning for years that the increasing size of vessels is leading to a higher accumulation of risk.[18] These fears are now being realised, potentially

18. Allianz. (2021) *The Suez Canal blockage and mega ship risks*. Available at: https://www.agcs.allianz.com/news-and-insights/expert-risk-articles/suez-canal-mega-ships.html

offsetting other long-term improvements in safety and risk management. Such ships generate economies of scale for ship owners but also a disproportionately greater cost for everyone when things go wrong.

Figure 9.1. The growing size of container ships (Allianz Global).

It is easy to see in hindsight that bigger ships and more frequent groundings in the Suez Canal increase both the likelihood and impact of such risks being realised. The question remains whether the MS Ever Given incident was a wake-up call for the shipping industry – and their customers. Car and computer makers were already straining from a global chip shortage in 2020 (but see how Toyota managed risk, below) and Californian ports were subsequently hit by backlogs and delay. The canal is an important route to transport oil and liquefied natural gas from the Middle East to Europe and there is also the potential for delayed shipments to technology and automotive companies as well. It appears that loss prevention measures have not kept pace with the growing size of ships. These are risks that need to be addressed from the design stage onwards – it is too late once the beast has grounded! With vessels capable of carrying 24,000 containers on the horizon future risks seem to be growing. Is risk management being compromised for the sake of bigger market share and profit margins?

So, what have these international crises got to do with public sector procurement? The impact of many of the highlighted incidents could have been reduced significantly if those creating or managing the risks had not only taken more time to consider what might go wrong, but also planned what to do in conjunction with both suppliers and customers – **prior to the event**. Partnership with those who share the risk or its outcomes, and a clear understanding of what risks are shared, is the key first step in this process.

Understand your suppliers

Partnerships demand mutual respect, understanding, openness and timely communications. Whether with a single supplier, multiple suppliers or through a managed solution, a thorough understanding – not only of priorities, vision and ethos, but also of areas of weakness or fragility – is essential. Sharing of business continuity plans provides reassurance and a mutual understanding of risks, assumptions, issues and dependencies. As we learn to live with the extended implications of the COVID-19 pandemic, it is reasonable to expect suppliers to revisit those business continuity plans, based on some of the lessons identified. For your key suppliers and contracts, you need to understand what sits behind the gloss of statements, promises and KPIs.

The Kraljic purchasing model mentioned in other chapters (See Chapter 4 – 'Know your supply chain', Chapter 7 – 'Think differently', Chapter 11 – 'Manage value' and Chapter 13 – 'Spend analysis') and shown in Figure 9.2, helps to explain where you should focus your efforts initially, from a supply chain perspective, whether this be for sources of supply or in respect of your contracts. For the public sector, profit is not necessarily the driving factor, but customer satisfaction and outcomes could be. The point is that this is not just an internal discussion that needs to take place, but also one you need to have with your suppliers and contractors. So, is procurement activity a subject for routine discussion at executive level or does it remain a department of business, supporting broader strategic and operational aims?

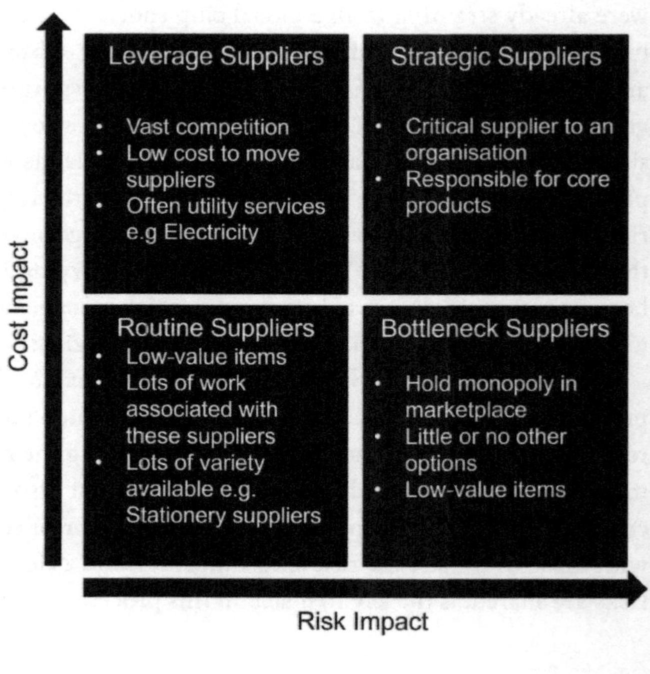

Figure 9.2. Kraljic model.

Procurement must be front and centre of discussions at a strategic level. This is not to say that all procurement activity demands such attention, but the approach should be proportionate to the perceived level of risk. Taking the Kraljic model, as a method of approach, we can then explore how to ensure key decision-makers are aware of supply chain risks. Table 9.1 provides an example of this approach.

Principles

Level	Focus	Observation	Action
Directors/senior managers	High risk, Impact, Customer satisfaction, Outcomes	Aware and engaged every 1-4 weeks but this is situation-dependent	Briefed on the procurement 'Top 10' but key to question/ challenge/seek clarifications and provide direction and guidance
Procurement professional and departmental heads	As above plus those assessed as medium risk, impact or profitability	Focus on the Top 10 but look ahead for potential promotion and relegation of issues	The filter by which issues are brought to executive level and actions are delegated
Service or departmental managers	Collectively own the contract register and detail future specifications	As above, but highlights requirements and proposes measures to meet future need	The key ground acting as the filter by which issues are brought to departmental head level

Table 9.1. Delegations.

Using the example of housing in the registered provider (RP) sector, whether you have outsourced your repair and maintenance functions, formed a joint venture or maintain a capability in-house, before the COVID-19 pandemic struck, did you know how much core or fast-moving inventory was held in terms of days', weeks' or months' worth of usage? Equally, did you know your partners' policy on resilience, contingency and risk and understand their supply chain? Ethical procurement demands an understanding of supply chains and employment policies of suppliers (and their suppliers too), to protect the rights of workers and to minimise reputational risk. Taking this principle forward, why wouldn't a RP or, in fact, any organisation in the private or public sector understand a supplier's supply chain and associated risks? After all, good partnerships only exist where both parties understand each other's strengths and weaknesses, don't they? This flows into effective contract management for mutual benefit. Look back at previous records of contract management discussions and see how often resilience, business continuity or risk were discussed and more importantly, were these areas covered on the standing agenda?

Where does risk sit?

Taking these points forward, businesses need to get into the mindset that risk is board-level business and is not just the remit of compliance, procurement, or any other departmental team. According to WBR Insights and Coupa, in its white paper, *Rethinking Risk and Opportunity in the Supply Chain*:[19]

> *'While the top supply chain risk concerns are operational risk and supplier risk, per the responses, CPOs report they lack confidence in identifying these risks in their supply chains. We also found that most CPOs do not think their functional leads and business units are properly equipped to manage risk. Almost all (99 per cent) of CPOs agree that risk should be the responsibility of the entire business, not just the risk and compliance teams. Yet they are not confident in their organizations' ability to manage risk, noting that IT, Procurement, Legal, and Finance are not adequately able to manage this risk.'*

In business, what we need to do is ingrain a culture of interest, challenge and, above all else, responsibility. Let's be frank; whilst you can delegate authority with appropriate responsibility to others, responsibility, ultimately, remains at the very top of the business, so let's take forward the methodology provided in Table 9.1.

Director/senior manager

Table 9.1 highlights some of the issues those who operate at executive level should be thinking about. Given the importance of procurement and supply chain management in sustaining businesses now and in the future, why wouldn't you take an interest in some of your key areas of procurement? It is simply not enough to lay the blame at your procurements officer's door when you have failed to get involved, or even shown a modicum of interest.

Experience tells us that things can and will go wrong and it is vital that those at board level provide clear and unambiguous direction and guidance to leaders and staff when they do. It is prudent to do so before any crash actually happens! Get involved and ask questions about routes to market, alternative routes to market (think contingency/resilience), especially once you've identified what your key contracts areas are (your 'top 10') and the broader business risks, which you will have already identified.

Drive lateral thinking and resilience planning in your leaders and management teams, so that, collectively, you can attempt to address identified areas of weakness or vulnerability. Encourage honesty and an open environment where questions and suggestions are considered positive approaches and not a reflection on an

---

19. Coupa. (2021) *The Year Ahead: How CPOs are Rethinking Their Supply Chains for 2021.* Available at: https://get.coupa.com/WBR-Survey-Report.html

individual or department. Think more broadly and ask what your competitors (especially private sector competitors) and peer organisations are doing and what challenges they face? When was the last time your business undertook a SWOT analysis, and do you really know where your weaknesses lie? Finally, which suppliers account for most of your key risk and what can you do to build in resilience or contingency with them and your organisation?

Procurement professional

You are charged with operational support by ensuring that those that deliver capability or effect are suitably resourced. You look up to board level for direction and guidance but also into the service delivery areas and understand what is going well and what is not. Those operating at board level will rely upon you for your expertise and recommendations, and you should never be afraid of imparting bad news.

The right thing to do is to highlight issues and then say or recommend what you're going to do about it. If areas need elevating for consideration at board level, then you are the conduit for this to happen; however, this is not all about what could go wrong. Good news and progress must never be forgotten and should also be publicised. You should bathe in the reflected light of the glory of your direct reports – not the other way round. This also provides assurance that capacity, ability and resourcefulness exist to highlight and *resolve* issues, rather than, simply, to report them.

Finally, think about driving decision-making at board level and what you can do for the broader benefit of the business. Perhaps, those at executive level would appreciate a procurement or commercial view of life – perhaps, a SWOT analysis may be one way to achieve this?

Contract/service manager

You may not think it at times, but you're the vital component in the machine of service delivery, along with members of your team. If you do not get what you need to meet commitments to your customers and people the whole organisation fails. You will have an intimate understanding of the challenges those at the vanguard of the business need and will be aware of the frustrations too. You maintain this awareness through your networks and relationships, as is explored in the first sections of this book on 'Awareness'. It is your role not only to highlight current issues, but also to think ahead.

You should be encouraging your teams to adopt the same mindset. Good ideas and solutions come from all aspects of the business, not just those that operate in more strategic positions. Get on the front foot and help the business help you by looking laterally and ahead. Team meetings are an excellent way in which to gain an accurate insight so periodically ask for ideas and thoughts about the business generally and whether anyone has any innovations they think would improve things. Sometimes, people may not be too keen to raise thoughts and ideas in public, so suggestions boxes or externally provided staff engagement surveys may be methods of generating responses.

Risk management process

So, what can we do about risk internally? The main tenets of risk management are summarised below. There are many views on how to manage and deal with risk but, in its broadest sense, these are:

1. Identify – what is it that may stop you doing what you need or want to do? These should be listed (prioritisation to follow).
2. Analyse – you need to understand and record the **likelihood** and **outcome** of each risk.
3. Evaluate and prioritise – this is where you consider the significance of the risk and prioritise accordingly.
4. Treat, mitigate or accept the risk – there are several actions here that might be involved: termination, mitigation, treatment, to tolerate or, in some cases, transfer the risk (although you will probably always own the consequences). It's important to recognise that sometimes all you can do is tolerate the risk; the key point being, at least, you've identified it, understand and accept the consequences.
5. Review – always undertake a periodic review of your risks.

There are many risk management templates available on the internet. Naturally, you may wish to adopt your own style and approach; however, by simply populating what you perceive to be your risks and the mitigating action you can take, you will help to frame the environment. Remember, it is not just your risks that you need to consider but also those of your suppliers and their suppliers.

What happens when a risk becomes an issue?

Once something happens, whether that is something that was identified as part of the risk management process or an unplanned event, how it is handled and how quickly, can be the difference between success or failure. As an example, across the tropics, monsoons are an annual or sometimes twice-yearly event. If you are charged with protecting life and property, there are mitigations you can take to help reduce the risk. Examples might be moving vulnerable people to safer areas or protecting property with flood defences. Once the monsoon occurs, your risk becomes an issue. Effective and timely decision-making, together with prioritising effort, demands good leadership but also excellent listening skills. All good contingency plans contain the need to form an effective decision-making body. So, dig out your business continuity plan and look for that key decision-making body and ensure it exists. If it doesn't, initiate it. Determine those key appointments needed to make good, rapid collaborative decisions and maintain up-to-date contact details. Don't wait for things to go wrong before scrabbling around looking for the people who will manage issues in an evolving and dynamic situation, often at short notice.

Summary

So, in understanding your suppliers' business continuity plans and the contractual framework in which they operate, where did your organisation sit in terms of priorities? If you did not know then and you still do not know the answer now, your relationship with supplier(s) was and continues to be sub-optimal; it is you holding the ultimate risk. The message is to get alongside your key suppliers (recognising that they may not be your largest) and work together, to share understanding and, more importantly, agree what action can be taken now as part of prudent preparation for the worst.

Do not wait for things to go wrong

Using your own experiences of the COVID-19 pandemic or other crises, did you experience stock-outs of key products or run close to exhausting avenues of supply? This is not to say that if you did you have failed, because shortages of some products were a fact of life across the globe. To mitigate totally against global supply chain challenges is probably near-on impossible and certainly unaffordable, but what you can do is think outside the box, identify what your core outputs and requirements are, and then begin to mitigate totally against potential risks, rather than ignore them or attempt to think they are someone else's problem.

And finally…

An extract from a CIPS article on 17 March 2021,[20] 10 years after the Fukushima disaster, prompts the following thought: do we ever truly learn about risk management and the implications of centralising production or storage in one area of the business? You could argue that it didn't work in 1982 and it doesn't appear to have worked in this example for many automotive manufacturers, despite the warning klaxons that rang around the globe after the 2011 Fukushima disaster. It is for you to decide.

20. Allen, A. (2021) *How natural disasters 'cascade through supply chains'*, Supply Management. Available at: https://www.cips.org/supply-management/news/2021/march/how-natural-disasters-cause-a-cascade-through-supply-chains/

Strained global semiconductor supply chains received another blow after it emerged a fire at a major semiconductor factory in Japan could be worse than first thought

Renesas Electronics Corp now believes damage from a fire at its chip-making plant was more extensive than initially believed, according to *Nikkei Asia*. Renesas initially reported the fire earlier this month had put 11 machines out of action, but unconfirmed reports now put that number at 17. The fire in northeast Japan started when a machine overheated due to an electrical fault. The company said its water supply and air conditioning were damaged in the blaze, which affected around 600 sq. metres of factory space. Renesas said it would take at least a month to resume production on its 300mm wafer line and that it could take considerably longer to replace damaged machines.

The company said: '*Although approximately two-thirds of the products manufactured within N3 Building can be alternatively produced in-house or in foundries, due to the recent increase in demand for semiconductors, the situation does not allow for all products to be immediately produced alternatively. We will ensure to make considerations to produce as many products as fast as we can.*' The development adds to the woes of the semiconductor supply chain, which is seeing a global shortage of chips disrupting production of cars and electronic devices.

Renesas accounts for 30 per cent of the global market for microcontroller units used in cars

One manufacturer appears to have learned from previous experience. As a top-selling automaker, Toyota seems like one of those companies that knows what it's doing.[21] It shouldn't be any surprise, then, that with the automotive industry struggling to cope with a global shortage of semiconductors,[22] the Japanese automaker is one of the few keeping its head above water. As reported by *Reuters*,[23] Toyota has been in a similar tight spot before.

Following the Fukushima nuclear disaster in 2011, the company was stricken by supply chain issues much like the ones other automakers are experiencing in 2021. This was, of course, a major setback for the world's largest car company at the time, so following the disaster, Toyota began to ask more of its suppliers. The company told its chip-manufacturing partners to stockpile two to six months of supply just in case — a demand that obviously paid dividends through proactive risk management.[24]

21. Gilboy, J. (2021) *Want Toyota's New 986-HP Hypercar? You Have to Answer These Questions First*, The Drive.
22. Stumpf, R. (2021) *Chip Shortage Continues to Wreak Havoc on New Car Production*, The Drive.
23. Shirouzu, N. (2021) *How Toyota thrives when the chips are down.*
24. Stumpf, R. (2021) *Automakers Can't Build Enough Cars Because We Bought Too Many Electronics During the Pandemic.*

Chapter 10 | Plan for Success, Prepare for Failure

'The optimist proclaims that we live in the best of all possible worlds; and the pessimist fears this is true.'

James Branch Cabell, *The Silver Stallion*

As we have already examined in this book, it may sound rather negative to focus on the worst that could happen at the start of a contract, relationship or tender, but it is time well spent. And, oxymoronic as it might sound, hoping for the best while simultaneously planning for the worst can be complementary activities. Success and failure, or opportunity and risk are, effectively, two sides of the same coin.

In Chapter 9 – 'Risk is Inevitable – Embrace It' we considered the need to accept and embrace risks and thereby prepare to avoid failure, and it is now time to turn our attention to issues and opportunities, and planning for success – things that we know, or should know, are coming our way and for which we need to plan. High-performing organisations will have seamless operational procedures that work effectively and efficiently, giving time and space for managers to do exactly this. Just having this capability and its associated culture and processes will reduce risk by raising the threshold at which risks become reality. Planning for and increasing agility, foresight and resilience will help to mitigate or overcome them if they do.

In an organisation, leaders should be collectively looking ahead to identify and plan, not only how they address any issues, but also how they maximise opportunities and innovation. Easy to say, but how do the best teams actually do it? As with other issues, we will look at this through several lenses, from the top to the bottom of the organisation. The first step is to assess how well this is happening in your organisation already. Start by seeing whether everyone in the value and delivery chain can answer 'yes' to *all* of the following?

1. Do you engage procurement professionals when you first identify an operational need within the organisation?
2. Do you know what changes are on the horizon that will impact your supply of essential/critical goods and services, and do your procurement colleagues know these too?
3. Are you confident that you are aware of all the opportunities that exist or that are emerging to do things differently, in a way that will deliver benefits?
4. Do you have a comprehensive, accurate contract register that enables you to plan ahead to recompete expiring contracts in enough time to implement a smooth transition between suppliers?
5. Do you have a resourced plan to manage routine business, emerging issues and secure the opportunities identified?
6. Do you understand the risks to that plan, through lack of resource or other unseen issues? Have you articulated that risk, up and down the management chain, in terms of likelihood and impact, and have you identified avoidance, mitigation, or resilience measures to manage that risk?

It would be nirvana if we could all tick these boxes so, realistically, what steps can the senior leaders, managers and professionals – from directors (all directors, not just the procurement director, if such a person exists in your organisation), procurement professional and internal customer or service manager – take to achieve this? In your commercial role, you should not only understand the requirements related to your role and position, but also those of the other individuals or departments. If they are not meeting these core requirements, it is up to you to lead, encourage, enlighten or persuade them to do so and start by setting your own example.

Lastly, it is worth understanding clearly that the process of planning needs to be part of the fabric of any organisation. There are only two set points in a plan – where you are now, and where you want to be – the plan suggests a route between the two. The first point changes automatically with time, and the last point changes as requirements, directives and circumstances dictate. It could, therefore, be said that the value of a *plan* is relatively limited, but the discipline of *planning* is vital and, because the environment changes, planning needs to be an ongoing process, *not* a one-off event. Proper, timely, prudent planning will therefore help prevent the organisation sailing blindly into the future, being driven by events rather than shaping them.

Director/senior manager

As a senior leader, you are responsible for creating a future vision, committing to that vision, and engaging your organisation from top to bottom to make it a reality. Your clear, understandable and achievable vision needs to be maintained and incorporated into business action, behaviour and culture throughout your organisation. It is your role to ensure that everyone in the procurement function understands the organisational vision and how their role and actions contribute. On an ongoing basis, you also have a key role in ensuring the procurement function is aware of emerging issues linked with the wider organisation. You must understand and harness the team members' collective professional expertise to achieve your organisational vision and effectively manage any issues outside their sphere of influence.

With that awareness of the organisation's strategic goals, opportunities and challenges, key stakeholders – who contribute to the supply of the goods and services that make your organisation a success – can align the supply chain to achieve those goals. Developing commercial arrangements and building strategic relationships do not happen overnight (except in an emergency or where the system has failed) and, therefore, the more time that everyone along the supply chain, including suppliers, have to plan, and the more transparent you can be, the better the results you should achieve.

You should be including procurement colleagues in the development of strategies and business cases to gain the full benefit of their professional expertise. They can help you to shape strategies by making them realistic, affordable and achievable so you can harness the best the market can offer. If a requirement for goods or services is presented late in the planning process, then all you can reasonably expect from procurement is a transactional service. Engaging your procurement colleagues earlier can allow them to make significant contributions to improve value for money and sustainability. You should be looking to your colleagues for two key inputs:

1. A challenge – if you need to be looking to source externally at all, or if you hold or should hold the expertise or resources internally.
2. Their insight including market knowledge, supplier engagement and awareness of new technology to shape your strategy and, where appropriate, your business case.

Opportunities and risks arise from external events as well as internal activities. You should look to your procurement colleagues to monitor the external environment and escalate the most significant issues to stakeholder groups, including to board level, where appropriate.

Procurement professional

A lack of early engagement from the business is one of the most common bugbears in a procurement function, with stakeholders contacting their procurement colleagues at the last minute. This restricts the procurement function to a transactional service and leaves no opportunity to add real value. The priority for procurement professionals, therefore, is to build the strongest relationships and reputation possible across your organisation so that stakeholders understand what you can offer. They need to realise the benefits of working with you and engaging with you to create a robust forward plan of upcoming activities. Whilst building an accurate forward plan can be time-consuming, maintaining it should become a core routine task, regularly engaging your stakeholders so that both parties can agree priorities for the upcoming programme of activity. It is essential that this is integrated with budgeting processes to ensure you have captured any significant capital projects that will require procurement support. Before commitments can be made to your stakeholders, you will need to ensure that you can appropriately resource the plan or, if you need to, allow you to engage senior managers to either secure additional resource or prioritise competing activities.

Once this forward plan is in place, it gives you the opportunity to operate at the next level and to start proactively working to identify issues and opportunities, planning for success.

There are multiple project management tools and techniques available to manage, monitor and control both individual procurement projects and your overall annual programme of work. Like all the best plans, they must not be so rigid that they are unable to flex and adapt to changing priorities. The key to managing these changes smoothly is to have an eye upwards and outwards so that you are well informed and connected and can take action early. Again, there are textbooks containing tools, such as SWOT analysis and STEEPLED, to help you identify these, but they need to be lived and practised, not just read. Regular monitoring of professional, industry, local and global publications will give you an early awareness of upcoming trends and issues while there is a wealth of resources and networks available to keep you at the cutting edge.

You also need strong supplier relationship management. Your strategic suppliers will only know what issues or opportunities may be relevant if they are aware of your goals. A relationship built on mutual benefit will then incentivise them to raise these issues with you.

You cannot sit comfortably in your 'professional bubble' and simply grind the handles of the procurement process, enjoying a happy and fruitful relationship with a growing list of competent suppliers. You need to understand the real needs of end-customers and those who deliver to them. You need to understand the emotional drivers that create need, before you can steer a professional course towards creating the outcomes that fulfil those needs. The only real way to do this is to communicate – speak with those end-customers and those who deliver the outcomes they need.

This knowledge, as well as accurate and timely management information, will support your conversations with service leads to develop prioritised work plans and will help your customers achieve their strategic goals whilst effectively juggling emerging issues.

At a more tactical level, don't forget the importance of planning each procurement, especially when navigating the Public Contracts Regulations 2015 (the PCR). A common understanding of the minimum timescales from the outset will avoid corner-cutting or non-compliance down the road. Effective planning enables you to work in partnership with your internal customer and access their expertise at key points of each procurement. If you need your customer's support with activities, such as attending workshops in the ROAD© process, facilitating site visits and evaluating tenders, then getting time set aside in your customer's diary early, and managing their expectations of the commitment required to get the best result, is a great start to a constructive working relationship.

Internal customer/service manager

Procurement teams are often asked at the last minute to buy a specific product or service when the internal customer has had a fairly fixed idea in their head of exactly what they want and from whom they would like to purchase it. The PCRs do not allow for this, but prescribing a known supplier also closes down the opportunity for any improved outcome. Open competition may result in the favoured supplier or solution, but will probably also offer better value for money or encourage them to innovate.

As the internal customer, you too should understand the organisation's vision and the part you play in it. With an understanding of what goods, works and services you need to undertake your role in achieving that vision, you should be able to plan ahead and engage your procurement colleagues in a timely manner – when you are considering a challenge and formulating a solution, rather than when you are trying to deliver it.

In the highest performing organisations, internal customers have a strategic relationship with their procurement colleagues. Some do this by allocating each area of the business a procurement 'business partner' who develops in-depth understanding of the function and supply chain while building a relationship of trust and collaboration with key stakeholders in that area.

In return for engaging with procurement in a timely way, you can expect your procurement colleagues to give strategic advice on sourcing strategies (buy, produce, re-engineer (reuse, recycle, repurpose), reorganise, outsource and so on), as well as share market knowledge and management information with you, so that you can work together to agree a prioritised work plan. They can offer you options and alternatives to step out of legacy processes and plan for change and continuous improvement.

Your day-to-day contact, with end-users and service deliverers, will help you understand what it is they actually need (as opposed to what they would like), and will often make you the first to be aware of issues or new opportunities. The skill that you need to develop and perfect is your ability to understand exactly what effect you want out of the procurement process – a clear definition of the desired outcome, not a specific piece of 'shiny' kit, or a service from a well-known 'safe' provider – and then communicate that effectively to your line management and procurement specialists.

The responsibility for delivering solutions to these requirements is shared. It is key that you share the intelligence you gather with your procurement colleagues and jointly agree any resulting actions. Procurement will rely on your technical expertise and operational knowledge and cannot take forward any initiative without your input. The best way to think of procurement is as an enabler that helps you achieve organisational goals in an efficient and compliant way. The procurement team members cannot do this on their own without your input, and you cannot achieve your goals without their insight and professional support.

Therefore, for individual procurements, you will need to have a timeline agreed with your procurement colleagues so that you can effectively manage your diary and invest the time required to get the outcome you need. If possible, establish a 'drum beat' of regular discussions at all levels across the delivery/procurement community to suit your operational tempo – it may be weekly at lower levels, monthly or quarterly, but the less frequent the discussions, the further out you should be looking. Do not just fire-fight current issues, however, have agenda items to look ahead at future requirements, horizon-scan for future opportunities or new technologies, and think about new ways of doing things. The risks of not effectively working together and planning are numerous and significant. It could result in there being no one available to run your tender, then, you lose your funding, your goods not arriving on time, exceeding your budget, exceeding your target carbon emissions, expensive and time-consuming legal challenge, and so on. Ultimately, it could result in you not achieving the outcomes that you are established to deliver, and the end-customers not getting the support they need and have directly or indirectly paid for.

The end-customer

If your organisation has succeeded, the end-customer may not see any difference; the service he or she expects will be delivered seamlessly and continually improve. End-customers will consider the service good value and have no cause for complaint. Your plans will have resulted in success.

We all accept, however, that this will not happen every time, and there is nothing more frustrating as a customer than asking for something and not knowing why that request has been refused, not getting the right outcome or perceiving that service levels are falling. It is even worse not to get the right outcome without explanation – frustration and, eventually, resentment will grow and any hard-won reputation of the providing organisation will take disproportionate time and effort to recover. This is often due, in no small part, to a lack of understanding about what is happening in the support and delivery chain, and why. It is, therefore, vital that all those involved in that support chain – from director through procurement professional and customer-facing service delivery teams – communicate to end-customers and each other future plans, the inevitable changes and, importantly, successes when they happen. They must keep the customer in the communication loop – for most readers, this isn't the Secret Service. Mistakes and unavoidable crises beyond your control will happen. It is worth reiterating that the procurement and delivery team should have the same interpretation and comprehension of what is happening, and they must also always speak the truth to the end-customers to maintain their confidence.

Part 3 | Manage Operations

Chapter 11 | Manage Value

'There is no victory at bargain basement prices.'
Dwight D. Eisenhower, 34th President
of the United States (1890 – 1969)

When Oscar Wilde wrote that a cynic was someone *'who knows the price of everything and the value of nothing'*, and contrasted him with a sentimentalist, *'who sees an absurd value in everything and doesn't know the market price of any single thing,'*[25] he was definitely on to something.

The two (price and value) are separate but inter-related concepts and strike at the heart of what it is to get the most 'bang for your buck' in terms of procurement. It's not just a simple case of looking at the price tag. To this end, we are going to look at how we manage value by not only focusing on lowest cost but considering the following:

1. Whole life costing (WLC)
2. Supplier Relationship Management (SRM)
3. Contract management (CM)

What does the word 'value' mean to you?

The word 'value' can have different meanings and interpretations to different people, and even the *Oxford English Dictionary* offers alternatives:

1. *'The desirability of a thing, often in respect of some property such as usefulness or exchangeability; worth, merit, or importance,'.*
2. *'reasonable or equivalent return; satisfaction' – VfM.*

In other words, value is in the eye of the beholder, and value is what you believe the product or service is worth to you, your organisation and end-user.

25. Wilde, O. (1892) *Lady Windermere's Fan.*

Value for money (VfM) can sometimes be confused with lowest cost – is there a difference?

One of the overriding requirements within public procurement is that all procurements must be based on VfM, which the government has defined as '*the best mix of quality and effectiveness for the least outlay over the period of the use of the goods or services bought*'.[26]

For some organisations, obtaining VfM is still defined by the ability to generate cost savings, to mitigate against cost increases and to drive down the unit cost through traditional win-lose approaches with their suppliers.

Although cost reduction (or even better, avoidance) strategies are important, some of the best organisations are now recognising the benefits of generating and managing value through the understanding of whole life costs, supplier relationship management and contract management. We will look briefly at all three areas and then discuss how the commercial roles within an organisation can support managing value.

Whole life costing (WLC)

WLC considers all the costs associated when making a purchase from pre-acquisition through to end of life including disposal, and is commonly referred to as 'cradle to grave'. See Figure 11.1. It also considers costs that are sometimes overlooked, including environmental and the social impact factors. For example, if a housing association were looking to invest in building new homes, would

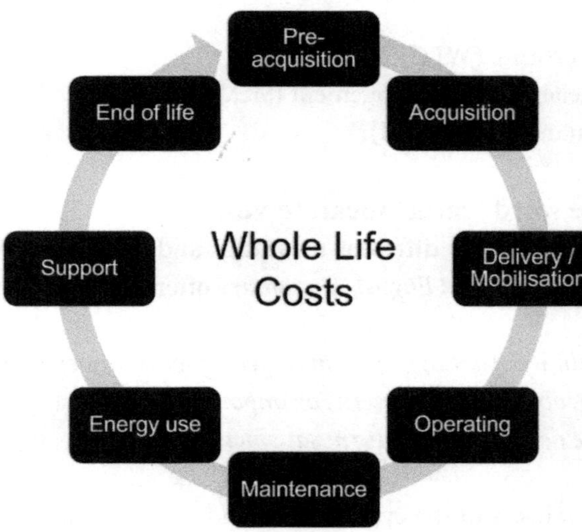

Figure 11.1. Whole life costs – an example.

26. Crown Commercial Service. (2021) *Public procurement policy.* Available at: https://www.gov.uk/guidance/public-sector-procurement-policy

it achieve 'best value' by only focusing on the headline lowest price? In this example, WLC not only considers the cost of materials, building contractors, specialist consultants and maintenance, but also the wider environmental and sustainability impact on the materials used to build the homes and the impact to residents.

Understanding these whole life costs will enable organisations to consider fully an optimum long-term value for money solution, rather than focusing on a short-term lowest cost solution.

Supplier relationship management (SRM)

What is SRM?

SRM is all about working more effectively and collaboratively with the organisation's key suppliers and developing a closer relationship, to deliver mutual benefits and maximise opportunities for delivering value.

What kind of a relationship do you have with your suppliers?

It is important to understand your supply base, so that your approach is tailored to the different kinds of suppliers, depending on the criticality of the goods or services they provide. Peter Kraljic created the Kraljic Portfolio Purchasing Model, as a method for segmenting the purchases or suppliers of a company, by dividing them into four classes, based on the importance of the purchases or suppliers, and the complexity or risk of the supply market. See Figure 11.2.

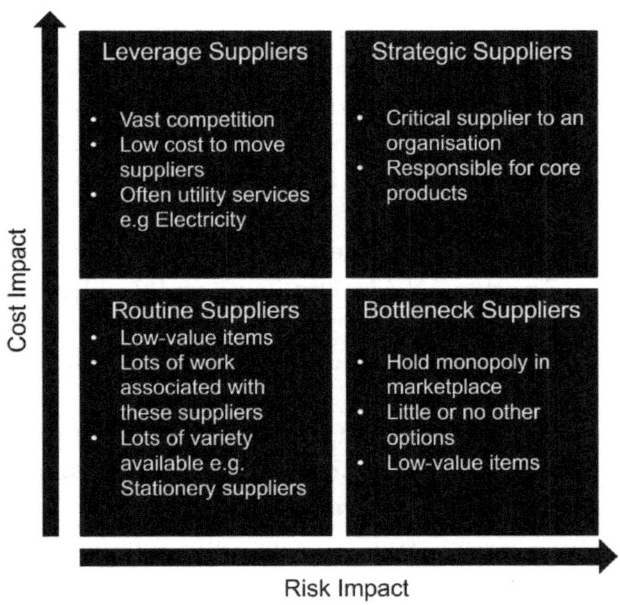

Figure 11.2. Kraljic model.

Some of the benefits realised from developing collaborative, close working relationships with those suppliers identified as strategic or key to an organisation include:

1. Best practice is shared – to drive efficiencies and improvements in supply.
2. Improved communication – making it mutual so the supplier is able to respond with any problems, allowing both parties to work together to resolve them.
3. Cost information exchange – increasing mutual benefits.
4. Risk management – how both parties can work together to improve the management of risk.
5. Increased trust and commitment.
6. Flexibility to meet fluctuating demands.
7. Non-price benefits, including sharing innovations.
8. Quality of service – improved performance, reliability and consistency.

The economic value of the supplier's non-price benefits (as described above) can greatly exceed the economic benefit realised from a supplier's price reduction.

This is explored more thoroughly in Chapter 4 – 'Know your supply chain' and Chapter 5 – 'Know the markets – ROAD© Part 2'.

Contract management

Whilst contract management is also covered in Chapter 17 – 'Don't let a contract and walk away', it is important to draw your attention to how value can be eroded through poor contract management. World Commerce & Contracting (in its previous incarnation as the International Association of Commerce and Contract Management ('the IACCM')) developed the 10 pitfalls to avoid in contracting, and where value can be lost; on average, most organisations lose more than 9 per cent of their overall contracts' value through these 10 pitfalls:

1. **Lack of clear scopes and goals** which can lead to claims or disputes and disrupted relationships. The then-IACCM identified that this affects at least 40 per cent of projects.
2. **The commercial team is engaged late in the day** – which may lead to the wrong commercial structure or terms.
3. **Failure to engage stakeholders** – external stakeholders are frequently left out and this may lead to misunderstanding, undermining the collaboration needed for value creation, innovation and trust.
4. **Protracted negotiations** – delays result in competitive exposure and extended time to bank revenue.

5. **Negotiations focus on the wrong terms and risk allocation** – which creates a more adversarial relationship, limiting the openness required to support innovation and value.
6. **Relationships lack flexibility and governance** – so that performance management becomes dominated by blame.
7. **Contracts are difficult to use or understand** – so that many people see the contract as only having relevance when there is a problem and also due to the complexity and language used, do not understand the contracts.
8. **Poor handover to implementation** – this means that commitments and obligations are missed.
9. **Limited use of contract technology** – this leads to inefficiency and loss of quality in performance and analysis.
10. **Weak post-award process governance** – this can result in repetitive issues and errors that cause value loss over time.

As an organisation, understanding the pitfalls you should avoid will enable you to mitigate the value lost, through poor contract management.

We have looked at three ways that value can be generated and can be managed in an organisation. So, how does your role support this?

Director/senior manager

As a director or senior manager, you are responsible for setting the vision and long-term goals of the organisation. This includes the strategy to achieve that vision. As we discussed earlier, cost-saving strategies are important; however, as demonstrated, recognising and understanding the importance of setting long-term value strategies could be much more beneficial to your organisation and the public purse. You should recognise that the role of the commercial function has moved from a short-term cost-saving activity, to a strategic function that can add value and drive non-monetary benefits. It can help the organisation to become a customer of choice with the right support from you. You should therefore consider the following:

1. Having a strategic approach to procurement.
2. Enabling the right people with the right skills to do the right work at the right time and in the right place.
3. Selecting the right systems, tools and technologies to deliver the best possible outcomes.
4. Understanding who your strategic suppliers are and encouraging more collaborative, performance-based relationships to deliver further value through SRM.

5. Embracing and communicating the importance of contract management competence to deliver the expected value from contracts.
6. Promoting the value of your purchasing function across the organisation so it is recognised for its expertise, and not used or seen as an 'admin' function.
7. Striving to be a 'customer of choice'.

Food for thought: finance is a standing agenda item on almost every Board or Executive meeting (i.e. how much have we got and how much have we spent?) How many have procurement or commercial on the agenda i.e. where did we spend it, on what and for what benefit?

Procurement professional

As a procurement professional, you should understand the value that procurement can offer, beyond savings, and how important it is to obtain VfM. Ask yourself this: Are you always invited to the table too late to add value? Are you seen as transactional, rather than strategic? What can you do to promote entrepreneurial purchasing and achieve a best VfM outcome, for the organisation and the end-user? You should be considering the following:

1. **Team working** – Build strong relationships with your stakeholders, to understand their requirements and that of the end-user and show them the benefits you can offer by working with you and engaging early on.
2. **Understand whole life costs** – As we discussed earlier, include all costs over time to understand the true costs of a purchase.
3. **Use data to drive more informed strategic sourcing** – Maintain spend and volume visibility (see Chapter 13 – 'Spend Analysis').
4. **Develop partnerships and longer-term collaboration with suppliers** – When appropriate, build partnering relationships to drive innovation, better quality and improved service offerings (See Chapter 4 – 'Know your supply chain', Chapter 5 – 'Know the markets – ROAD© Part 2' and Chapter 8 – 'Encourage innovation').
5. **Measure and evaluate performance** – Work with the supplier to determine the right and appropriate measurement using SMART metrics as described in Chapter 5 – 'Know the markets – ROAD© Part 2'.
6. **Consider the quality** – Ensure sufficient quality to meet the users' requirements whilst balancing whole life costs.
7. **Manage value through-life** – As described in Chapter 17 – 'Don't let a contract and walk away'.
8. **Keep it simple and clear** – Make the purchasing process for others as simple and efficient as possible.

Contract manager

As contract managers, you play a critical role in your organisation – having responsibility for administering your organisation's contracts in the most efficient and effective way and ensuring that the contracts deliver their full value. You are the direct link in dealing with contractors or suppliers and it is vital that you have a comprehensive understanding of the contracts you manage and the contractual agreements made between both parties.

Good contract managers know that once a contract has been signed, it does not mean that it should be filed away until something goes wrong; it should most definitely be a live and active document, that is understood inside and out.

Working with your procurement partner and other stakeholders, you will need to ensure you have been provided with a robust handover and have a clear understanding of the:

1. Legal obligations within the contract – so you appreciate fully what has been agreed between both parties.
2. Risk allocation – understand where the risks have been allocated and who is responsible for doing what to manage them.
3. Insurance and indemnity cover.
4. Opportunities to add value – innovation, service improvements, cost reductions, to name a few.
5. Scope or specification – know what the contract is delivering and when.
6. Performance measures – are these developed, appropriate and have they been agreed between the parties? And has a reporting/meeting cadence been established?
7. Change procedures – how are variations handled?
8. Incentivisation or risk and reward agreements – has anything been agreed to incentivise reduced cost, improved performance, early delivery, added social value and so on?

One of the most important aspects of your role is to develop and successfully manage relationships with your suppliers and stakeholders. You need to know what motivates your suppliers, who the decision-makers are and who the key points of contact are that you will liaise with on a regular basis.

Having understood the contract fully yourself, it is as vitally important that your supplier has interpreted the contract in the same way. Without this mutual understanding, contractual disputes could arise leading to poor performance, value leakage, increased costs, late deliveries and, ultimately, a breakdown in the relationship. Working in partnership with regular communication should help avoid, mitigate and alleviate these issues.

It is good practice at the end of the contract life to carry out a lessons-learned exercise to avoid repeating mistakes and move up the learning curve of 'what went well'.

A successful contract should deliver the best possible outcome for all parties and the end-user. Regardless of the size or complexity of the contract, this guidance is intended to set you and your contracts up for success.

Summary

The creation and management of value requires a focused, collaborative effort throughout the organisation. It is hoped that this chapter goes some way in explaining that, helping to shape your thoughts and helping you to generate ideas on how to be part of achieving the best value for money for your organisation and for end-users.

Chapter 12 | Use Legal Counsel Wisely

'Lawyers, I suppose, were children once.'
Charles Lamb, English essayist, poet and antiquarian (1775 – 1834)
Featured in Harper Lee's *To Kill a Mockingbird*

Asking a lawyer to tell you how to use them less or how to get the most out of them might seem a little bit like *'asking turkeys to vote for Christmas'*[27] but these suggestions are served generously...with a dollop of cranberry sauce on the side.

Be proactive not reactive

Lawyers are like friends – they don't just want to hear from you when you have a problem. So, try to get into the habit of using them to help you plan a piece of work to avert any issues. You can maximise the value of the piece of advice you're getting by, say, asking them whether a contract they've drafted can be turned into a template you could adapt later for a separate piece of work, to avoid confining the input to a one-off transaction and, in turn, reducing your reliance upon them in the future. That way, you could try to build up a precedent bank for you and your team. You may even gain so much confidence using documents at another time that you don't need their input. You are the one paying for the work so why not drive the outputs and optimise the value of that particular encounter? Think about whether counsel could offer some training for you and your team as part of the instruction.

To optimise the experience, try to be as specific as possible in the instructions you give to counsel as well. If your brief is too broad, it is possible that you won't get a specific enough answer to your question and you may, in turn, incur unnecessary additional costs for follow-up advice and clarification. Keep it short and precise.

27. This widely used maxim, about acting against one's own interests, is attributed to Penhaligon, D. (1977).

Every day's a school day

Another way of maximising the experience is to see whether there is something you can learn from the process. Is there something you don't know, some legal terminology you don't understand or a rationale for your lawyer's approach you'd like to have explained to you? Then ask. That way, you can build up your own and your team's expertise. Be curious – ask the solicitor what something means to increase your knowledge or understand why a particular course of action is proposed.

Tip: Although it may seem counter-intuitive, this is a scenario where youth, sometimes, outweighs experience – the younger lawyers still remember what they learnt at law school a few years ago; the so-called experienced, older, fustier and, no doubt, more expensive ones may have forgotten the intricacies of arcane pieces of law. Don't dismiss the value of using one of the more junior practitioners in a firm who may be young, eager to impress and has a lot to prove but is, fortuitously, less costly. Unlike Stella Artois, lawyers are not *reassuringly* expensive – they're simply expensive. Counsel can be bilingual too so, if you are puzzled by the language of a contract, ask them to translate a concept from legalese into plain English – if they can't explain a principle in simple terms, query whether they really understand it themselves and consider using someone else.

Irish playwright George Bernard Shaw coined the term '*conspiracies against the laity*'[28] for the techniques employed by the professions to safeguard their prestige, power and wealth. One of the sneakiest methods is the use of a secret lingo that is the exclusive preserve of the cognoscenti. Challenge that and don't be intimidated.

How *much*?

You may find it embarrassing to talk about money but it's good to understand from the outset how much a piece of advice or some drafting is going to cost, to avoid any unpleasant surprises. If you're using external lawyers, note that solicitors are subject to the Solicitors Regulation Authority's ('*the SRA's*') Price Transparency Rules, so they are obliged to publish price and service information on their websites, for certain areas of practice. They should also tell you how much they expect the work to cost at the start, keep you updated on spend and present a final bill. Of course, *should* and *do* are two very different concepts, and a practitioner can genuinely misjudge how much work is involved in a particular activity, while a case may become increasingly complicated over time. Hourly charges can quickly tot up, when the meter is running, especially if your lawyer

28. Shaw, G. B. (1906) *The Doctor's Dilemma*.

is using the antiquated six-minute increment method that some practitioners are still devoted to, so why not opt for one of the practices that will quote a fixed fee for undertaking a piece of work, so you can better budget for the instruction?

Tip: Try to avoid lawyers who use more creative methods of billing like the Norfolk solicitor, a few years ago, who charged the estates of dead clients by putting the files on the scales. He charged almost triple the fee, billed for thousands of pounds of work he'd not done and just dipped into the client accounts when he felt like it, rather than presenting final bills. Unsurprisingly and reassuringly, the man who said 'when you cost a file, you put it in your hand and weigh it' was struck off.

Whatever method of pricing that's used, you can always challenge your lawyer's bill. Try the firm's internal complaints procedure – which you should have been informed of when you originally instructed them – first. If this doesn't resolve the matter to your satisfaction, ask the Senior Courts Costs Office to make a 'detailed assessment' of your bill, as it has the discretion to reduce your bill, if it agrees it's too expensive.

Less is more

It's possible when you instruct counsel that you may not like the advice that you're given, either because you're dissuaded from following a possible course of action that you were intent on pursuing or because you feel that the advice you receive seems a little too concise. In these situations, you might think: What am I *actually* paying for? Sometimes, it's important to understand that there can be value in being told 'no' from a practitioner who has a wealth of experience in this area and can evaluate the prospects of your case or project. When legal advice is expensive and the response is succinct or advises against certain conduct, you may be dubious about its value. Sometimes, a £1,000 piece of advice at the beginning, cautioning against doing something or encouraging an alternative approach, may save you a lot more money further down the line, and it is the expertise that went into preparing that advice that you're paying for. A well-crafted paragraph may not look like a lot on paper, but it may reflect the years of knowledge and practical experience used to distil the information into a concise, palatable nugget.

There's no such thing as a free lunch

Not quite. Some law firms offer free lunch and learn sessions, breakfasts and webinars as part of their marketing strategy. You may gain insight for a current matter or knowledge for the future by attending one or more of these legal sessions. At the end of most of them, you may get a chance to ask questions, so you might be able to gain a cheeky bit of free advice, if your inquiry does not veer too far from the subject matter. Attendees often find that they can strike up a relationship with a lawyer (not *that* kind of relationship, which the rules once forbade but now tolerate) who's keen to market the firm and will give you *ad hoc* pieces of free advice in the hope that there may be a bigger piece of work in the future. Use this opportunity wisely, though, so that you don't feel a debt of gratitude to use them for paid advice and make it clear to them that there should be no expectations of that on their side.

Tip: Try not to corner a lawyer who you've just met socially and ask them for free legal advice, though. It's a pet hate. Would you ask a stylist you'd just run into at a party to whip out their scissors and trim your hair for nothing? No, we didn't think so.

If you can't beat 'em, join 'em

You may find yourself developing an increasing dependency on external legal advice and, although you've used all the tips above, the legal bill is still skyrocketing. Why not think about recruiting in-house counsel or developing skills internally within your existing staff? Is there an opportunity for someone in your team who may not have legal training or a legal background to build some basic legal knowledge or undertake a course of learning? That doesn't necessarily mean studying for a degree or going to law school. There is room for development through the Legal Executive route which facilitates a combination of work and study. Alternatively, you may be able to recruit someone into the team who isn't a qualified lawyer but has a legal qualification. Maybe you could offer an associate, a trainee or one of the new Trailblazer legal apprentices, at a legal firm that you use, a secondment for six months in-house. That way, you could negotiate an arrangement where the law firm pays for them and remains responsible as the employer, while you benefit from the expertise and the secondee, in turn, from the experience of being in your organization. Win, win, win.

It's not rocket science

Fans of the film *Legally Blonde* may recall that the lead character Elle Woods, when asked about her admission to Harvard Law School, quipped: '*What? Like it's hard.*' So, OK, law is *quite* complicated but 'it's not brain surgery', although it isn't a 'walk in the park' with 'a piece of cake' either. Ponder, before you get some advice or input, whether it's legal advice you're really looking for. Problems are often a tangle of issues and the answer, even when you engage a legal professional, may not be strictly legal in nature at all. Solutions often result from the alchemy of the Wisdom of Solomon, combined with pragmatism and common sense, so learn to look at problems yourself and see where you recognise the unfairness and what practical steps you could take to correct them. Risk assessment, another common theme, plays a part when you evaluate the impact of one course of action over another. Begin to identify trends in your procurement so you can become more proficient in undertaking repeated tasks. Learn from your mistakes and feed that back into your process. You may decide that you can very well resolve the matter yourself, without recourse to legal support.

I ♥ my lawyer

If you're using external counsel, how you find your lawyer will depend upon the circumstances. If you need legal counsel because of an existing or potentially contentious issue, you may find that you are afforded the discretion to look for a lawyer of your choice, if the matter falls under one of the exclusions listed under Regulation 10 of the Public Contracts Regulations 2015 ('*the PCR*') or '*specific exclusions for service contracts*'. Alternatively, you may be able to look for a lawyer for any other type of legal services, as anticipated by Regulation 74 and Schedule 3 of the PCR, or '*contracts for social and other specific services*'. You could instruct one of a range of legal practices that are run by public bodies, availing yourself of Regulation 12 of the PCR, which exempts certain contracts between contracting authorities or '*public contracts between entities within the public sector*'. Or you may opt to use one of the legal services frameworks, including those available through the Crown Commercial Service.

If you do have to use a lawyer, find one you like. Shop around. A good lawyer may be hard to come by and needs to model various traits which include strong communication skills, analytical prowess and creativity, in equal measure. Try to find somebody who is confident, as well as being your confidant, has a flair for problem-solving and offers good advice – effectively, someone who acts as your counsel and your counsellor. As with every sector, there is a range of quality and style. There are the good, the bad and the ugly; the risk-takers and the risk averse; bulls and bears; hawks and doves. What you probably want from the relationship is to find a lawyer who offers solutions for you with a can-do attitude; not one who is consistently saying 'no' but a trouble-shooter who offers workarounds like 'have you thought about doing this instead?'

Lawyers are like doctors in that, although they may have undergone broadly the same training, they will have developed different specialisms and, like physicians, their opinions and diagnoses may differ. Try to work with someone whose area of expertise is appropriate for your project or dispute and whose solution is most complementary and sympathetic to your needs.

Chambers and Partners, the Legal 500 or the Law Society's 'Find a Solicitor' function can help you locate individuals or firms by ranking or discipline. As in any sector, a charter mark is another useful guide of the standards you would hope to expect. For solicitors' firms, the Law Society uses Lexcel as the legal practice quality mark, which is awarded to firms that demonstrate stipulated levels for client care, compliance and practice management. But, as with everything, ask around too – word of mouth can be as good a recommendation as any.

When you do this, remember that the mantra of this book is 'private sector by head, public sector by heart', so don't be constrained by your habit of engaging legal counsel with public sector expertise only – someone who has experience of the cut and thrust of retail, FMCG, or even commercial disaster liability may be a better fit for your specific needs – as could one who has had a life before law.

Think about instructing a lawyer who may have had another career before qualifying into the legal profession and can, thus, bring added value and an understanding of the commercial world to what you're trying to achieve. Interrogate lawyers' backgrounds. Firms often publish on-line CVs for practitioners, and you can always resort to LinkedIn to check out an individual's previous jobs and professions. By way of example, a lawyer in a media organization who has previous experience as a journalist may understand better what the publication is trying to achieve, without curtailing the creativity and ambitions of its team of investigative reporters. That insight may ensure that the lawyer keeps writers the right side of the line, through careful editing, rather than scrapping their stories altogether. Similarly, if the lawyer you instruct has worked in your sector, in a different capacity, that person may have insight into your area of work and may understand your objectives better than a peer who has never had another job.

> *'The young man knows the rules but the old man knows the exceptions.'*
>
> Oliver Wendell Holmes, Jr. Former Associate Justice of the US Supreme Court (1841 – 1935)

The profession is brimming with people who have other areas of expertise, such as (East) German figure skater Katarina Witt – a star of the 1984 Sarajevo Winter Olympics alongside Jayne Torvill and Christopher Dean – while Michael 'Eddie the *legal* Eagle' Edwards, whose own Winter Olympics performance was, let's be honest, less dazzling, toyed with a career in the law for a while. On the other hand, be thankful for lawyers sage enough to have left the profession, when they realised their talents lay elsewhere, like actor Gerard Butler and singer Andrea Bocelli. Susan Calman, Rebel Wilson, Bob Mortimer and John Cleese are evidence that studying the law can be a pretty good warm-up for a career in comedy, though some might argue there are still some pretty funny people – some of them even frustrated poets – left in the profession.

You, on the other hand, might find that your use of counsel has been no laughing matter, in which case you should consider what steps you should take to address that. The regulators – in the case of solicitors, the SRA – impose the standards expected of practitioners. Generally, lawyers should act in the best interests of their clients, be open, honest and act with integrity. They should identify any conflicts of interest that would prejudice their ability to act for you, highlight any shortcomings in your case and keep you updated on progress as they go (there's no room for 'you never call, you never write' in the profession). If you feel that the lawyer you've instructed falls short of the standards you would expect, again you should start with the firm's internal complaints procedure and, if that doesn't satisfactorily resolve matters, consider whether the practitioner's conduct amounts to a regulatory issue that should be referred to the SRA (or another regulator, as appropriate) or whether it raises more serious matters that should be pursued through the courts or alternative dispute resolution. This, of course, is a last resort but most effective counsel will thank you for helping to maintain standards within the profession.

What could possibly go wrong?

Of course, it is much better to stave off a claim or complaint, through risk awareness, prudent preparation and by engaging counsel at an early stage – the kind of themes that abound in this book. This also chimes with the objective of achieving value for money because if you're incurring expense in resolving a dispute, the public is paying for that also. So, try thinking ahead. If you are tendering in an area where the goods or services are highly specialised, you or your staff might consider asking a law firm to produce bespoke terms, your budget permitting.

Give some thought before you tender to the implications of poor performance of the contract and whether standard liabilities (often set at no more than twice the contract value) would be sufficient if there were to be knock-on effects, such as lost income, that resulted from the supplier's errors or delays. If so, build the expectation of a higher cap on liability into the tender documents to set bidders' expectations early and to protect your position.

As with all steps of the process, engage lawyers early. Call them anything you want…but just call them.

A diligent brief in short *spell-he-can*
Draft bills as big as the pelican's.
Though your case he may *win–it's*
Made up of six minutes
Multiplied to the size of an elephant.
© 2022 Valentine

Chapter 13 | Spend Analysis

'Don't tell me where your priorities are. Show me where you spend your money and I'll tell you what they are.'

James W. Frick (1925 – 2014), former Vice President for public relations, alumni affairs and development at the University of Notre Dame

Procurement is centred on the acquisition of goods and services to meet business needs and deliver outcomes through an arrangement with suppliers under some form of contractual agreement. At the heart of all of this will be expenditure, which an organisation must control and monitor if it is going to survive. At this stage you need to separate budget management from spend analysis, because whilst they are both monitoring and analysing the same flow of funds, they are doing it for very different reasons and with different mindsets.

Budget management is concerned with ensuring that a purchase is from the correct budget, that sufficient funds exist and that the right suppliers are paid in a timely fashion. There is a lot more to it than that but, without wishing to alienate over-worked and underpaid budget managers, it will suffice for the purposes of this chapter.

Spend analysis looks backwards and considers *how* the money was spent in much more detail. Which suppliers were used? How was spend categorised? What percentage was under contract? Where was the money spent geographically? What size of companies were used? How many invoices were generated? Was spend spread appropriately within each category depending on the state of that market at the time? And so on. Spend analysis is not accountancy, it is detective work, and the conclusions drawn enable an organisation to adjust its spend behaviour in future for the good of the organisation's beneficiaries.

The first questions you need to answer are 'why conduct a spend analysis?' and, 'what are the potential benefits?'

Director/senior manager

As a director or senior manager there are some headline facts and figures you need at your fingertips to make decisions. Spend analysis is part of this management information (MI) feed and will enable you to understand not only the scale of your commercial activity, but also how effectively it is enabling departmental and organisational strategies and plans. A basic spend cube solution will provide this essential MI for you, whilst more advanced solutions will also enable you to manage commercial risk, monitor governance to ensure compliance with internal regulations and national and international law and identify opportunities for efficiencies.

Procurement professional

As a procurement professional spend analysis is both your quality assurance and your crystal ball. You need to be able to take the temperature regularly of the organisation's supply chain, and through spend analysis you will see where the external spend is being committed. Are those contracts you help set up being used or is there maverick spend occurring? Which departments are the key stakeholders for that review of legal services you were considering based on existing spend patterns? What is the carbon footprint of the organisation's supply chain? Do you need to adjust your forward plan and team size and skills based on historic spend activity? A procurement team operating without some form of spend analysis is operating blind and relying on luck rather than judgement.

Contract/service/delivery manager

As a contract manager spend analysis will complement and enhance the data you are already gathering on the performance of your contracts and suppliers. Historic data captured through spend analysis should not be a surprise to you, and often contract managers viewing spend data will get a warm feeling that everything is as it should be; however, you may notice that spend is higher than you anticipated because another department has been using your contract without authority, or perhaps you did not realise until now how many invoices that key supplier was submitting. Spend analysis alongside Category and Contract Management provides the additional management information needed to resolve issues or implement improvements based on factual historic spend data.

In summary, regardless of your role within the organisation, if you are in any way responsible for procurement then you will need to understand how the money is being spent above and beyond a budget management perspective. This crucial analysis is your assurance that best value is being achieved, that the end-customer's needs are being met, and that your commercial activity is compliant and legal. Without spend analysis your decisions are at best based on incomplete information and at worst an Onager estimate[29].

In this chapter we will explain the basics of how to conduct a spend analysis before detailing the responsibilities of Senior Management, Procurement and the Contract Managers.

Next, we will step through the basics of a spend analysis, but each and every one will be different depending on what the reason is for doing it. Some of these reasons are shown below.

Start

Decide *why* you are conducting this analysis as it will guide the actions that follow. If there is a blank sheet and the organisation has no specific requirements, gather everything and analyse it all! Usually, though an organisation has some idea what it wants, you can pick from a list of objectives including these common ones, which include wanting to:

1. Make efficiencies and spend less.
2. Identify who our strategic suppliers are.
3. Reduce the number of suppliers we deal with.
4. Know which suppliers produce the most invoices.
5. Ensure we are spending money locally/with small-to-medium sized enterprises (SMEs).
6. Understand which categories of spend we are spending our money on, and how this aligns to our Category Strategies (or if we want to use this analysis to start Category Management).
7. Know if we have leverage in our key markets, and if so, whether we are making the most of it.
8. Know if we are conducting our procurements in line with internal and external governance.
9. Identify if there is any evidence of fraud.

If in doubt, assume all of these and take every scrap of data available just in case, depending of course on how much time you have and what tools you have been given to do it. More on this later.

29. Onager = Wild Ass; Estimate = Guess.

Capture

Locate every system the organisation has with spend data in it and work with the various custodians to transfer it all across. Don't forget credit cards or procurement cards, and if there is a Contracts Register in place you should take that too. There is a minimum level of data required to enable an analysis, and you should always define this in a mandatory list of fields as follows:

1. Spend amount
2. Spend description
3. Supplier name
4. Transaction date

Without these you don't have a spend analysis. Remember, knowing what the objectives of this analysis are guides your data capture. If you need to report on how much spend has been committed in the local area you are clearly going to need the supplier's address.

It is worth taking a detour at this point to discuss influenceable spend as it is key to this entire process. The rationale for conducting this analysis is to identify potential improvements to the procurement process. Our focus is on money spent with third parties which we can influence in some way to improve commercial relationships, drive efficiencies, meet Corporate Social Responsibility (CSR) objectives and so on. We are therefore not interested in anything which we cannot influence, hence the term 'influenceable'. Pay, pensions, taxes, statutory fees to government bodies, loan repayments and most transfers to other public sector organisations are not something you can negotiate, so we won't focus on it. Most of these are easy for the suppliers of the data to strip out before it gets to you, but it won't always be 100 per cent successful, so you must be prepared to do this later with the assistance of the data owners. In some organisations they use the term 'impactable' rather than 'influenceable', but the concept is the same.

Data at this stage can be very raw and will often consist of many thousands of rows of spreadsheets. Less than 12 months of data and you won't have enough raw material with which to work. More than 24 months and you are now reaching so far into the past that much of what you see is no longer relevant. The only advantage to having more than 12 months of data is if the tool you are using for the analysis enables a year-on-year comparison, or if you know that the more recent year of spend data is not representative of a 'typical' year. Find all this out before you start, because this part can be time-consuming and test the patience of the data suppliers, so you really don't want to have to return and ask for more too many times!

Cleanse

Using clever software (quick and accurate, so preferable) or manually (slow and unreliable) the data is now checked for gaps, inconsistencies, accuracy and so on. A useful by-product of spend analysis is a data quality report, informing an organisation of the state of its supply chain data. To enable a meaningful analysis the data must be:

Complete. Blank fields can undermine your analysis, depending of course on whether they are on your mandatory list or not. Some blank fields can be populated through manual intervention or algorithms (the category of spend can be determined based on the supplier's name but it is not always 100 per cent accurate and is easily confused by companies with diverse and/or vast service offerings); others are a deal breaker and the resulting analysis will either be deficient or you must ask for better data.

Consistent. The way data has been captured will have a huge impact on consistency. If there is a good level of control at this stage then all will be well. If there is no control and a multitude of free agents have typed in what they want, there will be chaos. Much of this can be rectified with sophisticated algorithms which identify inconsistencies and fix them, but they are rarely 100 per cent accurate.

Accurate. Often as you analyse a dataset something does not feel right and you must always assume that no matter how sophisticated your tool you will never achieve 100 per cent accuracy. If something does not feel right then investigate it. If someone in the business knows more about that expenditure, supplier, category then seek their advice and do what you can to remedy the anomaly. We once discovered a transaction which was valued at £35,000,000, which stuck out like a sore thumb. After much investigation involving the department responsible and their finance team it transpired the decimal point was in the wrong place and it should have been £35,000.

This stage is crucial as the credibility of the analysis that follows is built upon it. Better to spend more time here ensuring the data is as robust as possible, than to present a flawed analysis later which has no value and is a waste of time.

Tools of the trade

It is worth pausing at this stage and having that conversation about the tools you are using. There really are three options:

Manual using spreadsheets and elbow grease. You can conduct a rudimentary spend analysis using the power of a spreadsheet, and a minimum level of analysis can be achieved through pivot tables or you could lay one of the many data visualisation tools on top. If there is no money to buy something better, time is not an issue and/or you have 20 people twiddling their thumbs then this will work. It takes an age to cleanse and categorise this way though, so only resort to this if there is no other way. Humans in the process also inevitably introduce errors, so good process and repeated peer checking should be considered.

Using the organisation's **ERP** system. If your organisation has implemented an ERP system then most of these come with some form of analytics tools built in or as an optional module. The advantage of this is that the data does not need to be transferred as in theory it is all in one place. The disadvantage is that often these ERP analytics tools are really only glorified spreadsheets, which once again you can plug in data visualisation if it is available or built in. If buying a specialist tool is not an option and your ERP system has the capability (and your data, good quality) it is the next best solution. The data will be refreshed automatically, available to all and it will take less time than the manual way with fewer tears.

Third party software. There is a buoyant market for spend analysis tools, and depending on your budget you really can pick from a wide range, considering what functionality you must have versus that which is nice to have. Most providers of these tools are also selling you some form of service too, so they will take your data, cleanse and categorise it and then provide you with a shiny visualisation which you can play tunes on to conduct your analysis. Some also provide a regular refresh to ensure the current data, and others come pre-loaded with market information or supplier data to enhance your analysis. Many are also provided by suppliers who have analysts and consultants who will do the analysis for you as a one-stop shop. This is by far the most desirable of the options, but it can also be the most expensive. It also allows management by exception of 'outlier' data and apparent anomalies.

Categorise

Most often when we refer to categorisation within a spend analysis, we are discussing the spend category or classification such as stationery, IT, agency staff or facilities management (FM). Categorisation can be applied to suppliers by Strategic Relationship Managers, contracts and buyers themselves as appropriate. These categories are usually applied to a transaction when it is first added to the finance system, but this is not always the case and will need to be rectified in the Cleanse stage if categorisation is to take place. Standard classifications exist (Proclass, UNSPSC) which are useful for benchmarking purposes and often an organisation will combine these common categories alongside those which are specific to its sector or organisation. If this analysis is for a single organisation and there is no requirement for any wider benchmarking, comparison or collaborative cross group analysis, this is not an issue. Consistent use of a common categorisation taxonomy is essential if the analysis involves more than one organisational dataset.

Once again, knowing the objectives of the analysis will guide you. If the final report must detail spend within the organisation's supplier categories of Gold, Silver and Bronze, then make sure this is included in the data before you start.

Analyse

This is the meat of the process where the analyst scrutinises the data, sorts and sifts it to spot patterns, inconsistencies or clues from which to draw observations for the report. This is part analytical, part experience and part creativity. If you have watched the 1999 film *The Matrix* this is the equivalent of the scene where Neo sees the matrix for the first time as a series of computer screens with alphanumeric characters cascading down and Cypher explains that '*All I see now is blonde, brunette, redhead.*' This is what an experienced spend analyst experiences when they are first presented with a serviceable dataset; it is no longer a series of transactions but instead it is an opportunity to consolidate contracts, identify an unmanaged supplier relationship, spot which departments are failing to use the organisational stationery contract and so on. As most organisations rarely carry out such an analysis this part can be the most daunting, and it why there is a market for specialists who can do it for you.

The objectives from the beginning will always be the first analyses completed, but here is a list of the most common which will be of interest to the recipient of a spend analysis report:

1. **How much was spent in the period and how does it split into influenceable and non-influenceable?** This gives us a key figure to work with and is crucial to determine the potential, size and effectiveness of our procurement function.

2. **What is the CAPEX/OPEX split?** Returning to budget management again for a moment, it is often good to know within the influenceable spend how much was spent on capital transactions and how much on operational. Understanding where an opportunity lies in this split and when a one-off capital expenditure may have skewed the dataset is crucial to developing an improvement plan. Also, the procurement of capital assets often requires a different approach to a different market than operational spend. In some organisations the funding streams may also be different, and any plans must take this into account.
3. **How many invoices were generated?** The definition of what constitutes an invoice is key, and you need to be clear from the outset whether this is counting the number of physical invoices issued by a supplier or the number of transactions also known as line items. Usually it is the latter, and the purpose of reporting this is to identify opportunities for improvement, as it takes time to process these invoices and the fewer the better. Be mindful that not all invoices are paper, and electronic invoices may not be flagged as such in the analysis.
4. **How many suppliers were used?** This is a line of enquiry in its own right which at the highest level indicates how many third parties the organisation purchased goods and/or services from. The key is to ensure this number is kept at the optimal level both organisation-wide and also within each of the spend categories, based on the state of the market and to meet any social value criteria.
5. **Who are the top suppliers by value?** Those suppliers considered most important to the organisation are not necessarily those with whom the most money is spent, but it is a good indicator to begin with. Some spend analysis tools will enable the production of a Kraljic Risk of Supply matrix, and where they don't it is a good analysis to include in your report.
6. **What is the percentage of spend on and off contract?** Another key measure of commercial health which can only be analysed and reported if the data was provided in the Capture stage.
7. **What are the top spend categories by value?** Decide by looking at the data whether you will focus on level 1 or 2, and how many categories you list. Consider what message this list is communicating, and consider also the percentage of the overall spend it represents. If the top five categories cover 80 per cent of the spend that will suffice, but if the spend is spread across a greater number of categories, you should use your own judgement.

Report

Naturally there will be some form of output at the end of the spend analysis, which could range from several people gathering round a screen, to a formal report in some format, to a presentation. What you report and how should be agreed at the beginning. There are many books and academic guides available on how to present data, but as a minimum we recommend:

1. Consider your original objective – did you meet it?
2. Consider your audience – will they understand your findings?
3. Be realistic. Spend data is never more than an indicator for further review. Only a foolhardy analyst sets sail in a boat made from their findings and expects to reach the opposite shore. Caveats and external reviewers are your friends.

One-off Spend Analysis vs Ongoing Refreshes

Organisations often commission or conduct a spend analysis, use the report, tick the box and don't think about it again. We recommend you conduct them regularly to ensure that all involved are receiving the latest information. Here is why, using a fishy analogy.

Imagine your spend data is a lake full of fish. This lake is fed from and indeed feeds multiple sources, so the fish in the lake are growing and changing through time. You sweep a net into the lake and land a fish and bring it to shore for analysis. You learn a lot from analysing this fish, and it forms a report which you now carry about with you to inform decisions within your organisation. However, within a few minutes of bringing it out of the lake the fish is dead, and what you learn is not going to change because the dead fish can only give you such information that it would reveal as it died. After a few months that dead fish is starting to smell a bit and people are starting to doubt the management information it represents, and after a few months more it is just bones and of no use at all. This is a one-off spend analysis.

Now imagine you don a scuba mask and stick your head directly into that lake we described earlier. You watch the fish and you report back on how the money is being spent, on what and with whom and you write a report. A week or a month later you stick your head back in and the lake has changed as the organisation continues to spend money or contracts expire or markets shift. You report back again and the information is fresh and relevant. This is an ongoing spend analysis. It takes some resource commitment and perhaps one of those third-party tools we mentioned earlier, but it is more effective, more relevant and nobody smells of dead fish.

Now we understand what a spend analysis is and how it is conducted we need to consider what is expected from different roles within an organisation:

Director/senior manager

There are some key facts you should know:

1. **The top level figures**. The organisational budget and how it splits into influenceable and non-influenceable and perhaps CAPEX and OPEX should be known to you.
2. **Your top suppliers**. Ten is a typical number, but you should know who they are and be assured that an appropriate contract is in place and that the relationship is being managed. They may be where you spend most or, in some circumstances, they may be the supplier of a critical service or goods that are essential to meet strategic priorities. If they are crucial to the success of your organisation then you may be involved in managing them personally. Leaders who are considered to be at the forefront of commercial awareness will not only know who their strategic suppliers are, but have been known to maintain a (regularly maintained) list on the wall of their office.
3. **What percentage is covered by contract**. You don't need to know the details of each and every contract, supplier and category, but you should know how well you are doing in this key measure. Every single commercial transaction should be covered by some form of contract, so anything below 100 per cent is a call for improvement. Within your organisation you should have your own target, and you need to know what that is so you can make the decisions and commit the resources to improve it where required.

If you don't know one or more of these then you need to speak with your procurement colleagues and get them to tell you. If they struggle to do this because there is no spend analysis tool in place or a spend analysis has not been conducted recently, then you have an opportunity to sponsor this and implement a solution. Without the key information here you can't possibly lead your organisation to achieve the commercial element of your organisational strategy. Without this you are almost definitely haemorrhaging money, providing a poor level of service to your end-customers and are highly likely to be *ultra vires*.[30]

30. LexisNexis. (2021). Literally means 'beyond the power'. It is used to describe an act which requires legal authority or power but is then completed outside of or without the requisite authority.

Procurement professional

The spend analysis is your tool and indeed the ability to analyse spend should be one of your skills. If a spend analysis is conducted within your organisation then you should either be personally involved in doing it, or be a key stakeholder in commissioning the third party who is. Finally, the outputs of a spend analysis indicate to you what is going well and what could be improved within the procurement function in your organisation.

You should know everything that the director/senior manager knows above. Further to this, you should also understand the origins of all of these figures. To reiterate:

1. **The top level figures**. The influenceable spend figure should be as familiar to you as your birthdate because this dictates the limits of your scope. Many procurement teams are not permitted or resourced to manage the entire influenceable amount, so you should understand what you influence, what you control directly, what you have no interest in controlling and what you wish you were influencing.
2. **Your top suppliers.** You should know who they are, what they supply, the status of the contract and have had some involvement in the tendering process. You may not be managing the contract but you know who is and you are assured that they are on top of it in accordance with an organisational contract management methodology.
3. **What percentage is covered by contract**. You are the custodian of the contracts register, so this number is another with which you should be intimately familiar. It is likely that the organisation is measuring your success by this number so you need to know what the target is and be working with your internal clients to improve it. For the transactions and arrangements which fall in the 'out of contract' percentage, you should be working with the relevant Contract Manager/Business Lead to rectify this and assure the organisation that any risk has been identified and dealt with.

Finally, another key element of a spend analysis is the potential opportunity for efficiencies within categories. Most third-party tools will include some form of arbitrary calculation based on the spend category, but as a procurement professional you will be able to work this out through analysis of the spend data. Opportunities to achieve greater value for money or cut costs are the equivalent of procurement medals. You need enough of these pinned to your chest to assure the organisation that you are as a minimum offsetting your costs, but typically covering and exceeding them.

Contract/service/delivery manager

If you have an intimate and in-depth knowledge of:

1. everything you buy
2. the suppliers you deal with
3. the contracts which are in place
4. appropriate plans and key performance indicators (KPIs) that are in place

all in accordance with a portfolio of plans and strategies (including category strategies) which ensure you are strategically and commercially aligned, then you probably won't be that excited by spend analysis. But you are a rare beast.

It is more likely that one or more of these statements do not apply to you, or perhaps you are considering how to improve your commercial contribution or respond to a change in the market you operate in? Now the spend analysis data is of use to you as there will be insights on fragmented approaches to key markets and categories, evidence that other areas of the business are undermining or not using your contracts as they should, and perhaps a realisation for the first time that one or more of your suppliers are submitting invoices far too frequently.

If a spend analysis is conducted then this is an opportunity for you to engage as a stakeholder, and assist with a review of the data to ensure it is accurate. This is an opportunity for you to identify any potential for consolidation either at a supplier, service or category level across the organisation.

Within your area you should know everything your senior manager and procurement lead knows about your suppliers and contracts but clearly your data should delve deeper to enable you to carry out your role. Part of your role is to understand the strategic importance of your supplier relationships within an organisational context and how they could be improved. You should be measuring this improvement through both the achievement of KPIs and in subsequent spend analyses.

Conclusion

In conclusion, any organisation which spends money with a third party in some form of commercial arrangement should periodically analyse their transactions in this way. Failure to do so or restricting this analysis to accountancy or budget management practices is the equivalent of viewing the world with one eye covered. Conducting regular spend analyses will enhance your knowledge of how organisational funds are being spent, which will in turn enable commercial improvement and mitigate risk. It is better to light a candle than to complain about the darkness, and spend analysis is a powerful candle.

Chapter 14 | Be Aware of the Signs of Fraud

'Fraud is often hard to uncover and can lie hidden for months or years before being discovered. During that time, fraud is like an infection eating away undetected until the pain is finally felt, but even then the financial and emotional impact continues.'

Martin T Biegelman, 'Faces of Fraud: Cases and Lessons from a Life Fighting Fraudsters'

There are different definitions for commercial fraud but this one stands out as it covers not only the 'what' but also the 'who':

'Procurement fraud is a deliberate deception intended to influence any stage of the procure-to-pay lifecycle in order to make a financial gain or cause a loss. It can be perpetrated by contractors or sub-contractors external to the organization, as well as staff within the organization'.[31]

Why should organisations care (and that includes directors, senior managers, purchasing professionals and contract managers, indeed, anyone involved in the commercial process)? Research shows that nearly 30 per cent of organisations experience commercial fraud[32] and such fraud undermines the hard work of everyone in the organisation. In the private sector, it may turn a profitable business into a less profitable or, indeed, unprofitable one, with potentially negative consequences for all of the employees. In public or non-profit sectors, the impact may go further than just the employees, with the fraud affecting the 'customers' such as the residents of a housing association or those supported by a charity. If

31. National Fraud Authority. (2011) *Procurement Fraud in the Public Sector.*
32. Niranjan, S. (2016) *Five Key Indicators of Procurement Fraud CPOs and Purchasing Heads Should Heed.*

fraud is impacting the cost of goods, services or works, then this is taking money or resources away from key services such as healthcare provision, education, support to vulnerable people and so on. It is also worth considering the impact of negative press, such as increased interest from regulators, as well as a breakdown in the trust and esteem held by the organisation. The organisation's reputation may have been built up over years and lost in a matter of weeks. In the public sector, it's taxpayers' money that's being lost and, arguably, there is a moral obligation on those responsible for public money to make best use of it.

Where does commercial fraud occur?

The opportunities for commercial fraud will vary from organisation to organisation. Some organisations will have tight controls and robust oversight processes, to minimise the likelihood of fraud as best demonstrated by players in the financial services market, such as banks. Some companies will have few formalised controls and, instead, rely upon the professionalism and law-abiding nature of their employees as may be evident in, say, start-ups. However, most organisations will be somewhere between the two.

Working through a typical purchasing process, let's look at some of the potential scenarios for fraud.

During the buying process

Conflicts of interest

All purchasing starts off with a requirement, the organisation needs to purchase goods or a service. There's nothing wrong with this, it is business-as-usual activity. At this point, the requisitioner could quite rightly ask (or check) whether there is a similar contract in place already or whether there's a history of the organisation having bought the goods or services. Such information might mean the new procurement is not required, after all, or it could help to inform the new procurement with insight on the market or on particular challenges. For example, there may only be a limited number of suppliers with the capability and/or capacity to meet the requirement.

Depending on the size of the organisation, there may be several people involved in developing the specification. Having a single person lead this stage of the process is not a red flag on its own; however, if that person is pushing for a particular company to be awarded the contract, then that may be worth investigating further. It may be that there is a positive history with that company, as it was a reliable supplier before. Of greater risk would be a conflict of interest, where the staff member (or a close relative) had a personal connection with the company. That could include being a former employee of the company or being married to a current employee, having a close personal friend in a senior position and so on. In this vein, there is the salutary tale of Thomas Marshall, who ran Baverstock Academy in Birmingham. An investigation found that he had hired his mother's consultancy firm without declaring it and did not follow proper recruitment procedures.[33]

If a particular company was used in the past, consider who the contract manager was at that time. If there's very little staff turnover, it may be the same employee that is involved again. What was the nature of the previous contract monitoring activity? Are there minutes from meetings in which the company was held to account for the contract deliverables, or were the meetings more informal, with no records kept, perhaps meeting routinely for lunch in a nice restaurant? An independent observer would clearly place more trust in the well-run contract management meetings, though that, in itself, is no guarantee that all is above board.

If there is a potential conflict, it is reasonable to expect the person to either have declared it formally already, or to raise it as a potential issue at the earliest opportunity. A conflict-of-interest policy is the first step in ensuring everyone is clear on what is required, and this can be backed up by a register to record declared conflicts of interest.

Bribery (kickbacks)

During the commercial process, many of the tender submissions should be treated as commercial-in-confidence. Possessing knowledge of a competitor's pricing submission would enable a company's own bid to be tailored to undercut it. Such information is, therefore, valuable, and the bigger the contract, the more valuable that information is. That value increases the opportunity for less scrupulous staff to leak the information for personal gain. The fact that so few commercial frauds are detected or result in successful prosecutions indicates that the fraudster is unlikely to suddenly display their new-found wealth. Indeed, the bribery may not even involve cash; it could be an invitation to corporate hospitality at a sporting event, the employment of a family member or a sizeable discount on the company's other products.

In short, the signs may be difficult to spot. Some people remain credible when lying and may hide behind their years of experience. Indeed, those frauds that are detected last an average of 14 months. In certain industries, the same staff are dealing with the same contractors year after year. Again, controls offer the means to reduce the likelihood of such fraud. If an organisation disables the USB ports on computers and monitors those emails sent with attachments to external addresses, it becomes difficult to share the information discretely. The

33. BBC. (2019) *Ex-head of Birmingham BBC documentary school banned.* Available at: https://www.bbc.co.uk/news/uk-england-birmingham-47497707

organisation can be upfront about its policy on minimising fraud, stating that all suspected incidences will be investigated fully and will lead to prosecution where possible. From the potential supplier's point of view, the need to preserve a trustworthy reputation should not be underestimated; however, it may be that there are sales incentives that unintentionally encourage rule-bending and poor practice for its own staff, thereby creating a fertile environment for fraud.

Restricting the number of suppliers

If there is a 'favoured' supplier, the requisitioner or, indeed, the purchasing officer could opt to reduce the number of suppliers in the frame so that the particular supplier has a greater chance of winning. This practice could be hidden behind such justifications as the specialist nature of the contract, the intent to focus on locally based small or medium-sized enterprises, or holding a restricted competition to save time. The likelihood of the favoured supplier being successful would be increased if the competition was chosen in the knowledge that other tenders would be uncompetitive. Taking this approach to another level would see the requisitioner pressing for a direct award to a particular supplier. There are circumstances in which direct awards are appropriate, but the purchasing manager must be satisfied that the motive for such an approach is legitimate and defensible.

Designing the specification

Another tactic that would favour a particular supplier is deliberately designing the specification to the benefit of a single supplier. For an engineering contract, this might include specifying a specialist welding capability against a limited or non-existent requirement. Again, an apparently credible case can be constructed to justify such a specification. The challenge is therefore for management to suspect an anomaly, question it and investigate.

Skewing the evaluation process

Assuming that the favoured company makes it through to the evaluation, there is further opportunity at this stage, for commercial fraud. The evaluation panel members should carry out their respective evaluations, in isolation of each other, only sharing their assessments at the moderation; however, shortcuts might be taken due to other pressing priorities. These could take the form of evaluators working through the tenders together at the same time, or one evaluator saying they will 'coordinate' on behalf of the whole panel. When staff are busy, they typically welcome such support and may not recognise the opportunity this presents an unscrupulous individual to influence the evaluation unfairly. That individual may be a strong character who unduly influences the other evaluators or may go further and change their comments and scores in a subtle manner that materially affects the outcome. The purchasing lead for the moderation must, therefore, ensure that the evaluation has been carried out properly with no 'helpful' shortcuts in the agreed process.

Bid-rigging schemes

Moving on from bribery caused by one or two rotten apples in an otherwise good organisation, bid-rigging schemes take the approach to commercial fraud to a different level. It is a point worth repeating that certain industries such as defence or construction see the same prime suppliers bidding for the same types of work time after time. Often there is a regular turnover of staff between these organisations and the same old faces keep reappearing. It is not then a huge leap for one enterprising individual to contact a trusted soul in a competitor organisation and arrange to collude on competing bids. Such instances are likely to start off small but, encouraged by their success, would quickly grow to larger contract amounts – the phenomenon of *creep* – and may ultimately involve more than two competitors. Clearly, none of this is good news for the contracting organisation which, even after going through a compliant purchasing process, sees the value of its contracts exceed the industry norms.

The organisations involved may have agreed to 'win' the work on a rotational basis, with some of the companies opting either to bid too highly or not bothering to bid at all. Such behaviours are essentially the creation of background noise, designed to mask the collusion under a veneer of an acceptable competitive process.

Post-contract award

So, our intrepid procurement professional has managed to navigate the potential pitfalls of the procurement process successfully, the contract has been awarded, and surely, it's time to relax with some business-as-usual contract monitoring activity? Unfortunately not, as the opportunities for procurement fraud remain a potential risk – *even* after contract award.

Mischarge schemes

Let's say that the winning supplier agreed to use 'Hyper Real' photographic paper as part of a publishing contract. Then, as a result of supply chain issues caused by an unforeseen event, a volcano, a blockage on the Suez Canal or a global pandemic, the supplier was instead forced to use 'Bob's Cheap Photo Paper' instead. If the supplier organisation is a bit stretched and not wholly organised, then the invoice may not be updated to reflect the material change to the contracted deliverables. Furthermore, once the error is spotted, three months have passed, so a blind eye is turned. The publisher, therefore, continues to pay for a superior product while receiving an inferior one. Even if the poor-quality paper does not react well with the adhesive holding the pages into books, what is going to alert the publisher to the issue? As the winning supplier has been the incumbent paper provider for years, the contract management meetings have long since lost any rigour and so the costs for the publisher rise, as do the margins for the paper supplier.

Post-contract fraud schemes are not limited to consumables. Organisations may charge for two maintenance staff for each call-out when, in fact, only one routinely attends. They may even invent call-outs and bill for work that never took place at all. Again, this may start off as a one-off but, over time, escalate into a significant fraud.

The resultant failings of the frauds detailed above raise some difficult questions for those involved. With the sub-standard paper, as more and more books fall apart and customer complaints rise, is the publisher listening to its customer base? If so, are these concerns acted upon? Is there any independent review of contract management activity, such as internal audit, to ensure that the contract management meetings are genuinely holding the supplier to account? If there are repeat call-outs for the same maintenance job, and progress is unusually slow, is there someone who notices that trend and investigates further?

The following cases provide good examples of different types of mischarging:[34, 35]

Barry Stannard, a former senior IT manager at Mid Essex Hospital Trust (MEHT), was found guilty of defrauding the Trust of over £800,000. In spite of submitting a nil return declaration of interests, he was actually the director of two companies that had received a large amount of money from the Trust over a 7-year period. No products or services invoiced for by these companies were ever provided to the NHS. The hundreds of invoices submitted by his own companies to MEHT were all individually for relatively modest amounts, meaning Stannard was authorised to sign them off without further checks. Concerns first arose after the Trust ran a data matching exercise on its payroll and accounts payable records, alongside Companies House records.

Russ Knowles, who worked for a consortium run by Kent County Council (KCC), bought energy in bulk for more than 120 public sector bodies. According to Kent Police, he secretly negotiated additional fees with a supplier and paid over £2m into a fraudulent account. KCC stated that the cash was being recovered. After the hearing, Det Con Mark Agnew said: '*This was an extremely daring abuse of position by Knowles. He deliberately set out to fraudulently secure a vast amount of money for himself.*'

34. NHS Counter Fraud Authority. (2021) *Essex IT manager pleads guilty to £800,000 NHS fraud*. Available at: https://cfa.nhs.uk/about-nhscfa/latest-news/essex-it-manager-pleads-guilty-to-fraud
35. BBC News. (2012) *Kent energy chief Ross Knowles jailed for £2m fraud*. Available at: https://www.bbc.co.uk/news/uk-england-kent-17937293

To prevent procurement fraud, what should be considered by whom?

Director/senior manager

From a senior executive's perspective, potential commercial fraud raises a number of questions, both within and outside the business. Cashflow is the lifeblood of any business, so the scale of the fraud may have a small or significant impact on the balance sheet. The senior management are those that are most likely to be concerned about the reputational impact, as they are the ones who may have to brief the media or face the regulator. Following the identification of the fraud, senior management should be taking the lead on ensuring appropriate controls are put in place to deny any future opportunity for a similar fraud. Indeed, the issue may prompt a wider review of controls with a broader scope than that single incidence.

Procurement professional

Procurement professionals are arguably best placed to recognise the warning signs of fraud. They have an element of independence from the requisitioner and, in order to deliver a compliant procurement, a valid reason to challenge on any areas where there is concern or ambiguity. The purchasing professional should be the person who is most aware of the potential consequences from taking short-cuts in the requisitioning process and should, therefore, insist that the correct process is followed. Applying the same professional approach to each procurement reduces the risk of fraud and sends out the message that poor professional practice will not be accommodated. There may be pressure to take shortcuts, particularly if what is being bought is to meet an urgent requirement. It is worth questioning whether the urgency is a result of poor planning on the requisitioner's part. If it is, then that may be a red flag worth considering.

Contract/service manager

The person responsible for the ongoing contract management activity is in a key position to identify fraudulent activity after the contract is awarded. Has the supplier delivered what has been contracted? If so, what evidence is there? Are the contract management meetings carried out in a professional manner or is there a drift towards informality and a less structured approach? Does the customer feedback align with the work that has been invoiced? If there's a disparity, then that warrants further investigation. Are the KPIs being met and the quality standards being adhered to? Not every performance dip will be a consequence of fraud but the contract manager should be close enough to the contractor to understand drops in performance against the broader context.

Conclusion

There is so much more that could be said about the more common examples of commercial fraud. Regrettably, the greater the opportunity and the greater the reward, the more incentive there is for the potential fraudster. There are some common themes to measure that can be taken to reduce the chances of fraud:

Tip-offs

A whopping 43 per cent of frauds are detected as a result of tip-offs or complaints.[36] To make the most of this opportunity, organisations should have well-publicised internal and external processes to capture these points. Make it easy for people to help the company by raising concerns; this needs to be backed up by a credible process for following up on such leads.

Disincentivise the fraudsters

In the same way that supermarkets have signs that say, 'All shoplifters will be prosecuted', make people think twice before committing fraud. Add the organisation's zero-fraud tolerance policy to the induction process for new joiners. Emphasise the severity of the response. In financial services, all potential employees undergo a Disclosure and Barring Service (DBS) check, and any history of fraud would effectively close off all opportunities for future employment across the whole sector.

Communication

That includes internally between different parts of the organisation, such as the finance and operations departments, to ensure invoices submitted match the work that has been completed.

Controls

Remove the opportunity for fraud. If only two people hold the safe combination for petty cash and there's a shortfall, either the control on who holds the safe combination has failed or one of the two has made an honest or dishonest mistake. If everyone knew that the combination for the safe was on a Post-it note under the telephone, to the right of the safe, establishing what had happened and catching the culprit would be considerably harder.

Follow the money

What proportion of the company's expenditure can be aligned against planned contract spend? If there are anomalies, what are the reasons for them? If certain members of staff are reluctant to explain what's going on, why is that? It's not their money so a reasonable level of transparency should be expected. Anomalies may be highlighted during spend analysis, which is discussed in the preceding Chapter 13 – 'Spend Analysis'.

---

36. Association of Certified Fraud Examiners. (2020) *Report to the Nations: 2020 Global Study on Occupational Fraud and Abuse*. Available at: https://www.acfe.com/report-to-the-nations/2020/

Part 4 | Be Responsible

Chapter 15 | Deliver Sustainable Outcomes

'How wonderful it is that nobody need wait a single moment before starting to improve the world.'

Anne Frank

'Be careful what you wish for, lest it come true!' is timeless advice from *Aesop's Fables*. It is also particularly instructive in how specific you have to be in articulating what it is you want to achieve with your supplier.

Consider two scenarios: The first, a council which lets a contract for a playground with an output-based specification that includes the latest and best playground equipment to be built in an area not far from a large housing development; the second, a council that lets a contract which defines the outcome as happy, active children. Which one of these is going to deliver long-term sustainable outcomes?

In this chapter, we explore the concept under the twin headings of outputs and sustainable outcomes. Take time to think about the outcome and not just the output. How does your organisation deliver sustainable outcomes?

Often, organisations are defined by reference to their outputs alone: the goods and services the organisation produces to meet the market's demand. It can be straightforward to pin down what outputs are needed to meet the needs of your customers, such as the first council in our scenario above; however, unlike outputs, outcomes are often forgotten or excluded from an organisation's strategic objectives. They are much harder to define and *even more* difficult to measure.

Society's demand for sustainable outcomes is justifiably increasing. Stakeholders do not simply expect goods and services, works or supplies that just meet their needs at the lowest price. Your customers, organisation partners or suppliers should also consider how every purchase or supply they make or every service that they consume is generating benefits – and not only for themselves as individuals or as an organisation. They now need to factor in what impact their actions have on the environment, the economy and society as a whole.

Furthermore, anyone who contributes to the organisation's internal function, such as employees or investors, should also think how everything they do could contribute to delivering sustainable outcomes to society as a whole.

As an organisation focused on increasing social value, you should take time to think not just about your outputs, but also how you deliver continuously sustainable outcomes. This should be a golden thread through your organisation's strategic objectives.

Sustainability[37] should be incorporated into every function of your organisation. To assess how these are effectively implemented, ask yourself the following questions for each of the three factors – Environmental, Social and Economic (ESE):

1. What ESE outcomes do we want to achieve as an organisation and what are the stakeholders' expectations?
2. How will the organisation drive optimal client ESE outcomes?
3. How can ESE outcomes be measured and evidenced?
4. After all, what do we gain from this?

Looking across the organisation, how do we actually achieve these outcomes?

Director/senior manager

As a senior leader you should have an in-depth understanding of the environmental, social and economic impact of your organisation's operations. Senior management support is crucial in driving the delivery of sustainable outcomes.

Looking inwards, you should ensure that your internal stakeholders understand the requirement and have the knowledge and tools to deliver continuously sustainable outcomes. You should embed and promote a culture that fosters sustainable outcomes throughout your organisation. Incorporate requirements to deliver sustainable outcomes on the management agenda across all your organisation's functions, including those in operations, marketing, human resources, finance and procurement.

Remember, you cannot do it all alone. Engaging your internal stakeholders in the decision-making process is crucial. People are more likely to be motivated and act in ways that can best help achieve the organisation's sustainable outcomes and objectives, when they are fully invested in achieving your vision. You should encourage an environment in which colleagues and partners are empowered to

37. Note: An example is primary schooling. The school can produce the best outputs. But it is only when those combine with local economic, social and environmental factors (such as family and housing conditions) that the educational outcome (i.e. fulfilling every child's potential) is produced.

contribute and help shape the organisation's strategic objectives. Points that you should consider include:

1. Are employees fully aware of your organisation's strategic objectives in terms of delivering sustainable outcomes? Do they understand how, at an operational and tactical level, their day-to-day work contributes to the overall strategic objectives of the organisation?
2. Are there channels within the organisation that encourage employee participation to generate ideas that can contribute to promoting sustainable outcomes? For example, cost saving or efficiency suggestions or service improvement ideas?
3. Do you promote innovation to break the cycle of outdated practices that result in poor sustainability outcomes?

You should ensure sustainable outcomes are demanded throughout your supply chain (internal and external) through your corporate governance framework by considering:

1. What products or services do you buy or commission?
2. What products or services can you produce or deliver as an organisation?
3. How do you shape the market and motivate suppliers to offer more sustainable products?
4. How will you select and contract-manage your suppliers to encourage sustainability?
5. How will you promote sustainable choices with your potential customers?

Focusing on external stakeholders, you should consider effective ways of promoting sustainable choices among your customers as well as with your suppliers. Look at sustainability from the customers' perspective and ask yourself:

1. Do you consult them and seek their opinions on your strategy?
2. Are they involved in agreeing the commissioning objectives for projects and programmes that may directly impact them (back to our story about the playground outcomes)?

You should also develop plans to shape the markets (see Chapter 5 – 'Know the markets – ROAD© Part 2') so that suppliers are aware of your needs and able to offer goods and services that contribute to your strategic objective of delivering sustainable outcomes. One of the ways of achieving this within your supply chain is by ensuring that your potential suppliers are involved from the pre-contract stages of the commercial process. They will then have a better understanding of your organisation's goals going forward. If they share your values (and why would you buy their goods and services if they did not?) they will be 'on board' and ensure that they offer more sustainable products, supporting your requirement for sustainable outcomes with each output they deliver. You should ensure that commercial and technical capability is connected as part of your organisation's sustainable procurement procedures to drive optimal client outcomes.

Procurement professional

Building stronger relationships with stakeholders while making sure that they have a clear understanding of what services the commercial function can offer to the organisation is central to the procurement function. It is a recurring theme in other chapters for good reason. A strong relationship will give you the opportunity to have regular contacts with your stakeholders. This should provide you with vital information and a broader understanding of the potential for future procurement requirements which will enable you to put together a procurement forward plan. You will then be well placed to engage with your stakeholders at the beginning of the purchasing cycle when needs are identified and specification determined.

You should not hesitate to challenge existing culture and/or practices within the organisation if they are not best practice or appropriate. Make sure that you offer your expertise so that any goods or services that are being procured are in alignment with the organisation's strategic objectives and will contribute to delivering sustainable outcomes. Some key points to consider include the following:

1. What is the whole life cost of the goods or services? Think about areas such as value for money, environmental, social and economic impact as well as the usual considerations (such as price, quality, lead time, functionality, compatibility, transactional costs and so on).
2. Is there a more sustainable version of the goods available within the marketplace?
3. Can services be delivered in a more sustainable way?
4. Is sustainability included as part of the service specification?
5. Who are the potential suppliers? Are they ethical providers who reflect your sustainability goals?
6. Does the specification make your expectations clear regarding the sustainability of the goods or services?

As a procurement professional, you would not be expected to draft the service specification, especially if you are not the subject matter expert; however, you can review or input into the service specifications from a purchasing or commercial point of view. Is the specification clear, accurate, up-to-date and complete? For example, do you engage a landscape gardener to cut grass and control weeds six times a year? Or do you contract for regular maintenance of grassed areas to ensure a certain aesthetic with measurable and qualitative standards (outputs vs outcomes)? Is the specification a combination of the function that needs to be performed (outputs) and the results (outcomes) that need to be met by the solution?

You should be confident and provide guidance or advice as well as undertaking commercial activities (such as market research insights to understand what the market currently offers) based on your commercial expertise. Another way of supporting the stakeholders in drafting sustainable service specifications is by ensuring that they are fully aware of your sustainable procurement strategic objectives or contract procedure rules or policy. Disseminating your sustainable procurement policy can help establish a clear commitment to action and ensures that service specifications are developed in such a way that they include sustainable outcomes. A sustainable procurement policy should highlight your organisation's top sustainability priorities and set your core procurement criteria. You might expect it to address such matters as emission reduction and waste minimisation, recycling, carbon footprints, low use or reuse of plastic and a process for conducting sustainability risk assessments for new contracts. Other ethical considerations, such as equality and diversity, child labour, forced labour, human trafficking, corruption, water monitoring, bribery and fraud could also be included.

There are many ways to successfully disseminate your sustainable procurement policy. Consider the following:

1. **Easy to read posters (online and hard copy)**: Summarising key areas in terms of sustainable outcomes to take into consideration when defining needs and determining specifications can be highlighted.
2. **Presentations**: Having a short presentation with your key stakeholders where you can talk about the sustainable procurement objectives and how, together, you can achieve these throughout the whole procurement process.
3. **Always refer to the policy and/or relevant legislation**: In every professional conversation (emails or meetings), you should always refer to the relevant procurement policy or legislation (including Procurement Policy Notes). Your stakeholders are reminded that there is a collective commitment to achieve agreed sustainable goals.
4. **Market shaping**: When engaging with the market via various procurement routes (such as Prior Information Notices (PINs), early market engagement

or a market warming exercise), you should ensure that you inform potential suppliers about your organisation's sustainable objectives and motivate suppliers to offer more sustainable products or services.

Contract/service/delivery manager

As a contract manager, you are responsible for the successful management of contracts, ensuring that each product or service contract you manage is contributing to delivering sustainable outcomes, not just to your organisation, but to the environment, the economy and society as a whole.

Some key points to consider include:

1. Do you involve your commercial colleagues at the beginning of the purchasing cycle (specifically, when defining needs and determining service specification)?
2. Do you bring suppliers' knowledge to the engineering of the service requirements (ensuring that they are on board with your organisation's strategic objectives for delivering sustainable outcomes)?
3. Do you keep your suppliers up to date with any changes in terms of the specification requirements for regular or ongoing contracts or one-off purchases, in line with the organisation's sustainability plans?

Do not be afraid of conflicting views from your commercial colleagues or even potential suppliers. Remember that it is not an easy task to bring about change in order to achieve sustainable outcomes. You should be prepared to accept feedback and be ready to challenge your own or internal standard practices. Consider the inclusion of robust sustainable outcomes when drafting service specifications. Some key recommendations include:

1. How does the particular service or product improve the economic, social and environmental wellbeing of the local area/society as a whole?
2. How does your specification facilitate the involvement of small and medium-sized enterprises and encourage local entrepreneurship, empower a particular minority group in your local community, promote human rights or combat unemployment?
3. Is there any added value (usually implicit) that the service would offer? What is it? Is this reflected in the service specification?
4. Do you hold category or supplier forums in which you can develop ongoing discussions with the suppliers, sharing best practice and giving them ideas regarding outcomes your organisation would like to deliver and how you

expect suppliers to work with you in achieving this? Note that, in some cases, suppliers would have built a close working relationship with the end-users/customers (for example in the health and social care sector); it is, therefore, to your advantage to treat all of your suppliers honourably so that you can work towards achieving and delivering sustainable outcomes together. The relationship should work mutually. This will eventually promote innovation, long-term and efficient savings, reducing adverse environmental impact on society as a whole.

What would that result in for the end-customer and society in general?

A satisfied customer is vital in order for your organisation to survive, whether you are public or private sector. End-users or customers do not simply expect high quality outputs at the most economical or lowest prices. They are becoming more socially and environmentally aware and expect organisations to deliver sustainable outcomes.

Most customers are thinking more ethically about their purchases and may be willing to pay more for goods or services that provide sustainable outcomes if the longer-term benefits are properly explained to them. Keeping your customers satisfied will put your organisation on a trajectory towards success. Delivering sustainable outcomes may require more investment upfront, but will deliver more social value from your organisation for the people it serves and the environment in which it operates. It will enable you to build a reputable brand image based on behaving responsibly and providing sustainable outcomes.

To sum up, delivering sustainable outcomes should form part of your key strategic objectives. It is not about outputs alone; it is also about looking beyond the traditional way of conducting business where simply meeting the needs of the customers at the lowest price is the main goal. Delivering sustainable outcomes is to your organisation's advantage: it promotes innovation which can help achieve best value for money; it reduces the adverse impact on the environment and the local economy; and it can promote resource efficiency for both suppliers and customers alike.

Chapter 16 | Be a Good Citizen

'Be the change you wish to see in the world.'
Mahatma Gandhi (1869 – 1948)

Let's think about that.

It may mean different things to different people, but it all comes down to thinking about other people, the impact your actions have upon them and being responsible for those actions. The impact of your actions should be positive, such as respect for others, being accountable, being honest and being moral.

Being a good citizen is something that can be delivered both professionally and personally, as these attributes are very transferable across both areas. For example, thinking about how your professional actions and decisions will have an impact on others. What does this mean from a commercial perspective?

Consider the following:

1. How can you leave a legacy that supports the communities in which you operate and how can you measure it?
2. When you are creating your specifications: Do you think about how your decisions will affect others? And are you being good citizens with the expected outcomes and deliverables?
3. Will this offer a safe and sustainable environment? Is it future proof? What will the end-user get out of this? How will this have an impact on the wider community? Do you feel good about it?

Both private and public sector organisations are under pressure from all stakeholders – regulators, customers, employees, investors and so on – to support the communities in which they operate. This is nothing new for the public sector whose *raison d'être* is to make a difference to the lives of those it serves. This objective was enshrined in law in 2012. The Public Services (Social Value) Act

2012 requires all public sector organisations, and their suppliers, to consider how the services that they commission and procure can improve the social, economic and environmental wellbeing of an area. For example, in Wales the Well-being of Future Generations (Wales) Act 2015 requires public bodies in Wales to think about the long-term impact of their social, cultural, environmental and economic decisions. This act is unique to Wales and offers a significant opportunity to make a long-lasting, positive change to current and future generations.

Delivering social value, like being a good citizen, cannot be done in isolation. You need to involve a wide variety of stakeholders, both internally and externally, particularly those individuals and groups who are most impacted by the outcome from a procurement exercise. You will need to understand the impact on those individuals or groups involved. Engaging with each of those stakeholder groups is essential so that you can understand their expectations and can design better services with their needs in mind, find new solutions to meet their needs or seek innovative solutions to their issues. You will also need to capture any changes that should be considered over the lifetime of the contract or project.

The Social Value Model, introduced in January 2021, includes stricter obligations on public sector organisations, in order to tackle key issues, such as rising social inequality, improving wellbeing, achieving net-zero emissions, promoting recovery from the COVID-19 pandemic, and links to the United Nations' Sustainable Development Goals. However, any social value requirements must be appropriate and proportionate to your overall business goals and objectives.

From a commercial perspective, you should ensure that you include social value in your tenders. Indeed, at the time of going to print, this is an obligation on all central government departments, their agencies and non-departmental public bodies and, undoubtedly, will become a requirement for all public sector bodies. This model provides a systematic and consistent way to evaluate the quality element of social value in bids, so that all suppliers, large and small, can successfully bid and provide an outline of what they can offer and how it will be delivered.

There are some key principles which everyone in the value and delivery chain should consider when delivering social value within your organisations:

1. Your social value themes and expectations need to be realistic and relevant. These will become apparent, as the engagement with the stakeholders evolves, but make sure you understand the reasons for the requirements and ensure that they are deliverable. For example, if a community wants a new fitness centre, as part of a development project and there is no budget available, nor suitable locations, this may not be achievable. You should

communicate why you believe this is not realistic or relevant and, if an alternative offer can be provided, this must be explored, such as support for a local bus service to a nearby centre.

2. From a supplier's perspective, don't over-offer or offer something that would be detrimental to the contract or could prove to be costly in monetary terms, as well as in credibility, that is it cannot be delivered, and credibility is lost. This could prove fatal and it may take time to recover from the experience, if recovery is possible at all. To extend the analogy, the solution might be to offer the bus service and, then, make the community pay to use it.
3. Keep proposals and plans open and transparent. Don't try and hide things; be honest. You will be found out and all credibility will be lost. Trust is vital. Ensure trust is maintained by making communication suitable to all parties, so there is no ambiguity or misunderstanding. For example, as outlined above, sharing that you will provide the service without advising there is a cost implication.
4. A key thing is to make sure all social value and community benefits are future-proof and relevant to the term of the contract and to adapt to any changes, where required, like many have done, due to the challenges faced by the COVID-19 pandemic, that we have all faced in our private as well as working lives.

These matters are so important, as we saw when the Queen delivered her speech to the Houses of Parliament in May 2021.[38] In this vein, Guy Battle, Social Value Portal CEO, identified some key takeaways, for public procurers and suppliers, that show how we can expect to level up our communities and help them to recover and renew:[39]

1. 'How can you support a national recovery from the [COVID-19] pandemic that makes the UK stronger, healthier and more prosperous than before?
2. How do your proposals level up opportunities, across all parts of the UK, supporting jobs, businesses and economic growth and addressing the impact of the [COVID-19] pandemic on public services?
3. How can you support the health and wellbeing of the nation, including tackling obesity and improving mental health?

38. *Queen's Speech 2021*. Available at: https://www.gov.uk/government/speeches/queens-speech-2021
39. Social Value Portal. (2021) *The Queen's Speech Supporting Social Value*. Available at: https://socialvalueportal.com/queens-speech-supporting-social-value

4. How can investment into large infrastructure projects unlock more social value for communities, including proposals to transform connectivity, by rail and bus and to extend 5G mobile coverage and gigabit-capable broadband?
5. How can you support a lifetime skills guarantee?
6. What steps are you taking to invest in new green industries to create jobs, whilst protecting the environment?'

The first stage of the process is to develop your social value strategy. Don't panic though; when trying to decide what is social value and how you design your strategy, there are tools to help. There is the Social Value Strategy which is based on National TOMs (*no, not tomatoes*). The National TOMs Framework has been designed around five principal themes, 20 core outcomes and 48 core measures to assist with the implementation of your strategy, as follows:

Themes – The overarching strategic themes that an organisation is looking to pursue

Outcomes – The objectives or goals that an organisation is looking to achieve that will contribute to the theme

Measures – The measures that can be used to assess whether these outcomes have been achieved. For the National TOMs Framework, these are action-based and represent activities that a supplier could complete to support a particular desired outcome.

For Welsh public sector bodies, the National TOMs Wales are more akin to a social charter or manifesto than a measurement framework designed to allow organisations to assess their social value contribution to the Well-being of Future Generations (Wales) Act 2015.

Your strategy should be classed as the golden thread of your business, to maximise benefits throughout the life-cycle of its development, and plan and develop strategy, from the board to directors and stakeholders, to the commercial team, suppliers and so on, and the end goal must be clear and relevant at each stage. Delivery of your social value strategy should be considered as part of daily business management and, as part of your personal life, as being a good citizen. It should be at the forefront of how you conduct your business and yourself. This can even start with a 'Good Morning' to the team or when you collect your drink from the coffee shop.

Once the strategy is established, you need to ensure that you are delivering against it, and that it is creating social value for society, making the difference and delivering the impact desired. It will need to be reviewed to ensure it is achievable and relevant and, again, it must be future-proof.

This should also be part of your overall business strategy and, in particular, your procurement strategy. You should ensure that social value is captured during your tender process, so that you can give your suppliers the opportunity to be part of the wider picture and to offer community benefits or add value to a contract. This can be evaluated with other areas of the tender, although evaluation criteria must be clear and not ambiguous, and any social value requested must be relevant to the contract delivery.

This is supported by the creation of the government's Procurement Policy Note PPN06/20 – taking account of social value in the award of central government contracts – which confirms the importance of social value, as part of the tender process[40].

Even though at the time of going to press, this is only mandatory for central government contracts, this is likely to become best practice across the public sector. With the reform of public sector procurement and the introduction of the new Procurement Bill, the requirement that all public sector buyers *consider* 'social value', when selecting suppliers, is likely to become standard practice – even obligatory – for all public sector buyers and it could even become part of private sector standard practice, in the future.

Management of social value should be something you strive to do in partnership with your suppliers and should not be one-sided. Your suppliers are vital in the delivery of your contracts so remember to make the social value objective achievable within your tender, so it does not deter suppliers from bidding, as they cannot meet the requirements. Also, you need to ensure you consider the impact of these requests upon sole traders and small and medium-sized enterprises who may lack the wherewithal to deliver this added value.

Social value looks beyond the price and considers the overall benefit to the community. This can be an extremely forward-thinking opportunity to change the way business is done. It is a breath of fresh air in the world of commerce and can be seen as both a positive, from an employer of choice perspective, as well as an organisation which is good to do business with, from a market perspective.

All in all, social value is here to stay, so embrace it and, like being a good citizen, it will give you a feel-good factor which can be infectious. Who knows where it could lead?

---

40. Cabinet Office and Department for Digital, Culture, Media & Sport. (2020) *Procurement Policy Note 06/20 – taking account of social value in the award of central government contracts.* Available at: https://www.gov.uk/government/publications/procurement-policy-note-0620-taking-account-of-social-value-in-the-award-of-central-government-contracts

Part 5 | Contract Management

Chapter 17 | Don't Let a Contract and Walk Away

'There must be a beginning of any great matter, but the continuing unto the end until it be thoroughly finished yields the true glory.'

Sir Francis Drake (1540 – 1596)

Active management of contracts and the search for continuous improvement

Whilst other chapters have focused on addressing the correct behaviours and questions you should be asking yourself on the journey to establish the very best contract for your organisation, this one highlights the importance of the journey post-contract signature. That's right! The job isn't over once the contract has been signed. The best organisations will ensure this is just the beginning and adopt the right actions to ensure they don't 'let and forget'.

It is too common a pitfall that excellent procurement projects which incorporated supply chain expertise, excellent stakeholder engagement, proper market research and genuine innovation are then wasted because post-contract signature, the agreements are placed in a drawer to gather dust. How can your organisation avoid this and ensure that all the hard work and effort invested upfront actually comes to fruition throughout the lifetime of the contract? Consider the following:

1. How much time does your organisation invest prior to contract signature versus post contract signature?
2. How often are you holding contract management meetings, particularly with your strategically important suppliers? When, if ever, are you involving procurement professionals in these meetings?
3. Are these contract management meetings only focused on what is going wrong with the contract?

4. Do you have a dedicated contract manager for all your strategically important contracts?
5. Do you regularly track key performance indicators (KPIs) and are you utilising them to truly add value?
6. Can you be confident that the benefits (including financial and social value) that you believed would be achieved at the outset of the contract have been genuinely realised?

Once the contract has been signed, it isn't just up to the contract manager to make sure the outcomes we so carefully crafted in the requirement are realised. As we have seen throughout the procurement process from genesis to contract let, it is a team effort. So, do the team slap the contract manager on the back and head home for tea and medals? Not quite. The team responsibilities continue unabated, as we show below.

Director/senior manager

As a director or senior manager, you should be confident that your strategically important contracts are being actively managed. You are unlikely to be directly involved in the management of the contracts yourself, but you should support and empower your team(s) to be able to do this effectively. For those core contracts that your organisation relies upon you should know who the third-party supplier is and who your internal contract manager is.

In your position, you will have a very clear view on what your organisation's overall strategic goals are. Ask yourself: 'How many of these goals rely upon strong performance from a third-party supplier?' You may surprise yourself at how many of them do. It is your role to embed a culture that respects and places appropriate emphasis on the importance of proper contract management. You should therefore be doing the following:

1. Ensure that all strategically important contracts have an internal contract manager assigned to them. **Note:** 'Strategically important' is not confined to high-value contracts. Certainly, some may be high-value but not all of them will be. What about that out-of-hours call handling contract that only costs £50,000 per year? If that supplier failed tomorrow, would your organisation be in danger of not providing the service levels expected by your customers?
2. Provide continuous training to those contract managers to ensure they are empowered to perform their role to the best of their abilities. Contract management has shown it does (and will continuously) evolve. Gone are the days when suppliers are only called in for a meeting when something goes wrong. In fact, quite the opposite should be true. A contract that is

being effectively managed should rarely need to address poor performance because it is being managed proactively. It is therefore vitally important that you equip your team(s) with the latest knowledge and tools to allow them to undertake contract management properly. Furthermore, when aiming to secure funding for any training remember that World Commerce & Contracting (previously the International Association for Contract & Commercial Management) states that poor contract management costs companies 9 per cent of their annual revenue. This is a significant figure so why not invest in getting it right?

3. Be a contract management champion! We all know that people listen to the messages that come 'from the top down.' Use your position to ensure that you stress how vitally important proper contract management is. You will come across doubters along the way, but use your role as an opportunity to demonstrate and then demand the right attitudes.

Procurement professional

As a procurement professional, you may think that you have done your bit as soon as the contract is signed. Although the majority of your work has been done once you hand that shiny new contract over to the operational side of your business, there are still some key aspects of contract management you should be getting involved in.

Once the contract begins, as a procurement professional you are likely to be involved in procuring/managing new tendering projects; however, the best procurement professionals in high-performing organisations will be adopting a 'category management' approach. This means that for those strategically important contracts we addressed earlier, you should be involved 'cradle to grave', that is right from the business opportunity being born through to the contract's end of life. Why get involved in managing the contracts and what should you be focusing on?

As the procurement professional involved in the project 'cradle to grave,' you are in a unique position to know exactly what the appointed supplier stated in its tender response. We have all probably fallen victim to a supplier promising the world during its tender submissions (often utilising completely separate teams to present the bid versus the operational team who then actually delivers it) only for it to then not deliver the specified outcomes. Having the benefit of being involved in the tender process means you can add real value for the appointed contract manager during performance meetings/reviews, and your presence will also keep the supplier on its toes.

Suppliers will often not expect procurement professionals to be present in the operational contract management meeting. Indeed, on multiple occasions I have walked into such meetings as a procurement officer and have been met with comments such as, 'Oh. We didn't know YOU were coming' or 'We didn't expect YOU to be in these meetings.' It is no surprise that I have, therefore, witnessed a correlation between procurement presence in contract management meetings and those particular suppliers improving performance against key performance indicators (KPIs). Suppliers know that procurement professionals involved in the tendering exercise are very likely to know the 'in*s* and out*s*' of the contracts and, more specifically, what was promised at the tendering stage. They consequently raise their game when it comes to contract performance. Finally, as a procurement professional, you should categorically be involved in contract management for strategically important agreements. This will allow you to learn lessons about what is going well in the contract and what isn't so positive, knowledge that will be key when it comes to re-procuring in the future. No contract will ever be perfect; however, the aim should be to make every new iteration of a contract an improvement on the last.

Most procurement professionals will need to obtain business approval before awarding a contract. This usually takes the form of an 'award report' or 'business case outcome'. It is standard practice that these reports will document the perceived benefits of the new contract. This could include multiple elements but, most commonly, it will cover financial savings, social value outcomes and any other noteworthy efficiencies such as an improved specification or quicker delivery times. The key word here is that the report details *perceived* benefits. Too often, procurement professionals draft an 'award report' specifying they will achieve X, Y and Z benefits, only to then hand over the contract to the operational teams and never actually track whether the *perceived* benefits materialised. Benefits realisation should be a high priority in all organisations for procurement professionals – especially on those strategically important contracts where you should be tracking and reporting back to the business on what benefits have actually been achieved.

Contract/service/delivery manager

As a contract manager who may be responsible for one or more contracts you should be truly living and breathing the in*s* and out*s* of your agreements. You should be the go-to person in your organisation for these contracts and the supplier(s) associated with them. With your granular understanding of the specification, objectives (and their associated timescales) and risks, you should have your finger on the pulse and know whether the contract is delivering as expected or not. Too often, contracts are procured and then put away in a cupboard or drawer to gather dust. Instead, in high-performing organisations, they will be well-thumbed documents that are routinely referred to during business-as-usual, not just if something goes wrong. So, as a contract manager, what should you be doing to maximise performance and outputs?

As specified earlier, you should be holding regular contract management meetings with suppliers and key stakeholders from your business. As the contract manager, you should be chairing and driving these meetings. How often should you be having these sessions? It really depends on the complexity and strategic importance of the contracts. As an average, once every quarter is a good target. Ensure you do not employ the 'old school' approach to contract management where you only invite the supplier in when something goes wrong and you need to 'give them a talking to'. The best organisations, with the smoothest running contracts achieving their set objectives, will be the ones that proactively have contract management meetings which are used to promote good news stories, positive performance results and to address and encourage further innovation, best practice and areas for further continuous improvement. Remember, the contract can act as a 'stick' if the supplier is not delivering, but equally as important is the 'carrot' or reward mechanism. Too often, contract managers are overly focused on perfecting 'get out' clauses or mechanisms for punishing poor supplier performance such as liquidated damages, termination and so on. However, what about the opposite; providing incentives and rewards to the supplier for meeting or exceeding expectations? Additional bonuses or early payments are just two ways of achieving this and you'll certainly find that the promise of a 'carrot' drives much better performance than fear of the 'stick.'

KPIs should be central to your contract management meetings. These are a critical measuring tool to determine how well the contract is performing against the six 'rights of procurement' (product, place, time, price, quality, quantity)[41]. KPIs measure the contract, the supplier and client/lead organisation. High-performing organisations will not only measure what is easy; they should measure what is important, what relates to a potential improvement or potential problem, and ensure it is within the authority and ability of those involved. The most critical word here is 'key'. Contracts can have upwards of 15 KPIs. This is too resource-intensive for supplier and client to manage reasonably and creates a negative culture in which an industry is made purely out of KPI reporting. Best practice suggests that 6 KPIs is the magic number; pick what is critical to track performance against the contract and go with that. KPIs should usually be considered early in the procurement process (although some highly complex projects will see them finalised during the inception phase) as your procurement

41. Some texts quote the '5 Rights' and include the 'Right Supplier' in the list, but in our experience, if you have the 6 Rights listed above, the Right Supplier will be found.

plan/business case is created, incorporated into the tender process, bound within the contract and then monitored/reported on by you throughout the contract term. Choosing which KPIs are appropriate for your contract is naturally dependent on what you are procuring; however, a few common examples include order accuracy percentage, on-time delivery, return reasons, customer satisfaction score, budgeted spend versus actual spend and first-time fix rate. All KPI measures must be SMART (See Chapter 5 – 'Know the markets – ROAD© Part 2').

The best organisations will ensure that 80 per cent of their time is invested upstream (prior to contract signature), so that everything on the journey to letting a contract is in place, including market research, specification writing, contract formulation and tendering. This takes significant time to do properly. However, when done correctly, this will mean that the remaining 20 per cent of time can be dedicated to downstream activity. This is where the contract manager will really come to the fore and ensure that the contract is being delivered as efficiently as possible, reporting on performance and exploring potential innovation and service improvements. Too many organisations fall into the trap of rushing into the actual tendering element. They hurry to get a contract awarded without investing the appropriate time upfront: 20 per cent of their time is invested upstream but, then, a mammoth 80 per cent of their time will be focused on downstream activities and the majority of this will not be on value-adding activities. Instead, it will be spent trying to make a sub-optimal contract run smoothly, frustrating the contract manager, the supplier, the organisation as a whole and, importantly, the end-user. Ensure your organisation plans properly, engages procurement professionals as early on as possible, and invests the right amount of time in getting the contract right. This will mean that your 20 per cent downstream activities, as a contract manager, will be a lot more effective and add genuine value.

A bonus fourth piece of advice for contract managers is to create and utilise a 'contract management summary'. This is also sometimes known as a 'contract management manual' or 'contract operating manual'. This should be an operational template or plan which details all the key information you will need to know or refer to during the life of the contract. Many contract documents are detailed and unavoidably long. Locating the information you need can often be frustrating and time-consuming as you thumb through page after page. You can avoid this by creating a 'contract management summary'. Pull out the information that is vital to you such as contract start and end dates, key personnel for both parties including their contact details, budgetary information, payment plans and KPIs. Put this information into a one- to two-page document. You can then quickly access this when you need to without having to search aimlessly through a series of large contractual files. Another key benefit of this approach is that you don't have to amend the contract when, for example, key personnel change.

What will all the above lead to for the end-customer?

If the various personnel identified above start adopting the behaviours and approaches outlined, your organisation will be well on the way to undertaking contract management in an effective way. The above isn't an exhaustive approach to contract management; far from it. However, these fundamentals will mean that your customers should start to experience benefits.

What are these benefits? Well, they could be numerous and varying. A lot depends on whether you are managing a contract that benefits internal customers (operational teams/colleagues) or external customers. Either way, proper contract management should achieve and improve the 3 'Es' which are:

1. **Economies** – Saving money OR doing more for the same or, even better, less.
2. **Efficiencies** – Making that contract run as smoothly as possible will result in efficiencies where goods, services or works can be delivered more quickly and/or to a higher standard.
3. **Effectiveness** – Ensuring the contract delivers the outcomes it set out to achieve. This is where KPIs are king; make sure that the contract is a tool that allows your customers to get the results they need.

Acknowledgements

The creation of a book, particularly through the collaboration of multiple individuals, requires the acknowledgement of input and assistance from a wide variety of people and organisations. It will be clear through the reading of this book that we are indebted to the many mentors in a wide variety of organisations for helping us to shape our collective thoughts on the commercial world and procurement, as well as those who supported us in bringing this book together.

The individuals who helped develop this manuscript deserve special recognition. I appreciate the efforts of all my co-authors, without whom this book would not have got off the ground. Too many to name here, however, you can read a short biography for each of the authors in the next section. I am in awe of their enthusiasm and passion for this project and their individual and collective knowledge and experience of the commercial world and procurement.

Our valuable clients (past and present) provided us with ample opportunity to hone our commercial skills in practice. We have learnt from each and every assignment.

Thank you to **Rona Bassett** and **Ailsa Maclean** for co-ordinating the whole team and keeping us on track and on schedule, in spite of our efforts.

Thank you to **Spencer Hill** whose cartoons make one either chuckle, scratch one's head or wonder if he is on a different planet. He tried very hard to steer us into creating a commercial and procurement cartoon strip and I'm sure his next book will be much anticipated.

We are indebted to **Chris Markey** for undertaking the task of editing all the chapters and ensuring consistency across the various writing styles and natural enthusiasms of the authors. He was very diligent in taking our individual submissions and converting them into a readable manuscript.

Suzanna Hinnell and **Suzy Valentine** for undertaking the first edit and bringing the best out of the manuscript.

We appreciate the efforts of the editorial staff at **The Self-Publishing Partnership Limited (SPP)** who have guided and supported us in understanding the publishing process and providing encouragement, proofreading and formatting of the manuscript. In particular **Garry Manning** was instrumental in us choosing SPP, **Douglas Walker** worked with us at every step patiently answering all of our many questions and **Frances Prior-Reeves** expertly led the editorial and final design phase.

Our thanks to **Paul Alexander** for his interest in and willingness to provide the foreword.

Thanks, as always, to **Joanne Hanson-Young,** whose constant support and encouragement, throughout the process, kept us all sane.

Finally, thanks to Hasbro Inc., current owner of the *Operation* game, which inspired the cover and to Cavity Sam, its main protagonist, whose image we used. It seems apposite that a game based on helping those in need should be used as a model for encouraging use of the best elements of the respective sectors: Private by Head, Public by Heart. As Winnie the Pooh, another hero, acknowledged: '*Sometimes the smallest things take up the most space in your heart.*'

Ian McPherson OBE BEM FCIPS

About the Authors

The authors are all current or former consultants of 4C Associates Ltd. Together, they have more than 400 years of experience in commercial, procurement and supply chain roles in the public and private sectors.

Alan Pibworth MCIPS MSc BSc (Hons) CCMP has extensive supply chain management experience across the world, delivering sustainable and enduring logistics solutions for geographically isolated detachments and deployed elements. He has been the principal logistics and personnel officer, supporting over 2,000 UK personnel in Southeast Asia and has trekked the foothills of Nepal for the Gurkha Welfare Trust.

Andrea Djordjevic MCIPS has over 15 years' public sector experience within local government, higher education and the housing sector. However, a career highlight within the private sector is that she met Norman Wisdom and served *Take That* their breakfast *(Relight my Frier!)* A memorable achievement of hers was introducing e-auctions for taxi and bus services and making savings of £500,000 per year.

Chris Markey FCMI FCILT was a Logistics Officer in the RAF for 35 years. As Deputy Commander of Joint Logistics during the last Gulf War in 2003, his team of 9000+ service, civilian and contract personnel successfully supported all warfighting and humanitarian operations from Jordan in the West to Oman in the East. He has been a logistics and supply chain consultant and mentor for the last decade, working with industry, defence and academia.

Chris Robinson MCIPS is a national award-winning procurement professional with over 15 years' public sector experience across several local authorities and higher education organisations. He has been responsible for procurements including light rail acquisitions and major works construction packages. He is an accredited CIPS lecturer delivering the qualification to students for the last eight years.

Dez Waterworth Prince2 MSP Scrum-Master BSc (Hons) CCMP has worked in a multitude of sectors in analytical and leadership roles within the UK and across Europe. Career highlights include redesigning the customer self-serve online portal for RAC's personal breakdown members and reviewing their onward travel product to highlight potential cost savings of circa £250,000 per year.

Edward Pinkard MInstLM CCMP has over 20 years' experience of delivering change and transformation within both public and private sector settings. He recently led the delivery of the States of Guernsey's five-year Financial Transformation Programme delivering savings of more than £25m per year across the island's public services.

Emma Pearce MCIPS CCMP CMI is a procurement professional with over 15 years' experience working within the public and private sector. She has supported high profile infrastructure projects (£100m+) for Jaguar Land Rover and successfully developed and implemented a strategically important construction framework (>£200m) for one of the leading housing associations in the country.

Grace McCalla BSc (Hons) DIS accomplished a first-class honours degree in Mathematics with Economics and was awarded the Mathematics Placement Prize for her placement year submission. Whilst working in the private sector, she achieved savings in excess of £1.6m during the financial year of the COVID-19 pandemic.

Ian A McPherson OBE BEM FCIPS is an acclaimed practitioner in his field of complete supply chain management, following a successful career as a military logistician. He has taught smart procurement on the Acquisition Management MSc at Cranfield University and has been a visiting lecturer in both the USA and France. Ian's achievements include being an Executive Board member of the Single Source Regulations Office for the MOD from its inception and leading the review and establishment of a new Ministry in the Government of South Sudan.

Malcolm McFarlane DipA Log MCIPS CCMP has extensive experience of supply chain, contract and supplier management developed during a long career in the Army and roles in cyber programme management, TV production and holiday complex management in Spain. Malcolm is an elected Community Councillor and chairs a local environmental charity organisation.

Paul Naismith MSc BA (Hons) CMILT MCIPS CCMP has over 20 years' experience in operational logistics, supply chain management and procurement. Much of that experience was gained in the Royal Air Force, where he was a Logistics Officer. He has continued his service as a Royal Logistic Corps Officer in the Army Reserve.

Paul White MBA MCIPS has experience in many public and private sector leadership roles in local government, housing, higher education and the rail sector; he has recently focused on organisational change. His key achievements include setting up a large public sector shared service and helping create a successful public sector joint venture company where he was a Non-Executive Director.

Rona Bassett MCIPS MSP CCMP BSc (Hons) has served both public and private sector clients on a variety of transformation and change projects, including several cross-sector collaborative commercial and procurement programmes. She was the technical lead for review of the Department for International Development's approach to its £1.4 billion yearly spend through commercial suppliers.

Ross Hodgkins MCIPS BA (Hons) CCMP is a self-confessed 'procurement nerd,' who has a unique passion for everything public sector. The Public Contracts Regulations 2015 and their application in Housing Associations would be his specialist subject on Mastermind! He won 'Colleague of the Year' in his previous role for his work on a business-wide transformation project for a housing association with 1,200 colleagues.

Spencer Hill MCIPS CCMP has worked in or around the public sector for over 30 years (except for the brief period when he concentrated on cartooning and illustration, published a couple of books and taught at the London Art College). He has advised and served in central and local government, charities and education to improve services through operational procurements and (his favourite) spend analysis.

Suzanna Hinnell CCMP BA (Hons) MCIPS has experience in many public and private sector roles including working for the MOD, local government and an IT start-up. Her greatest achievements are delivering £2m/year savings for an NDPB by designing and implementing a new commercial solution for agency staff and leading a Russell Group university's procurement service through the COVID-19 pandemic.

Suzy Valentine MA (Cantab) (First Class) LLM CCMP is an award-winning journalist-turned-lawyer who draws from her commercial and creative experience in Europe, North America and the Far East. She has undertaken trial observation overseas, leading to a challenge to the European Court of Human Rights, assisted on the Grenfell Tower Inquiry, and has written for the Daily Mail, Sunday Mirror and Reuters.

Yannick Mukendi BSc (Hons) PGDip is a passionate procurement professional with extensive public sector procurement and commissioning experience. He has a substantial track record of strategically sourcing a variety of high-profile projects, including specialised public health schemes, social care services, social housing services and a variety of European Regional Development-funded projects.

4C provides expertise across all areas of cost transformation and procurement, for leading organisations in all market sectors. Its services range from strategy development through to implementation of procurement services focusing on outcomes. 4C works with its clients to deliver sustainable, cost-effective supplier contracts, enhancing end-customer engagement and the delivery of results.

4C is regularly selected to undertake major projects with blue-chip clients and public sector bodies, due to its innovative approach and high-level talent. 4C offers an unrivalled combination of capabilities, geared towards resolving complex challenges and delivering sustainable, tangible results.

As well as serving a diverse range of private sector clients, 4C has a proven track record of supporting a panoply of public sector bodies including but not limited to housing associations, higher and further education, schools and an array of government departments, to effectively manage and improve their procurement and supply chain resources effectively.

Appendix | Glossary

Glossary of tools, techniques, models and processes

Tool, technique, process or model	Brief Description
Buurtzorg	An alternative to Traditional Top Down Public Service Delivery involving radical organisational restructuring. https://buurtzorg.org.uk/
CAPEX	Capital Expenditure.
Casserole Club	An alternative to Traditional Top Down Public Service Delivery involving peer-to-peer support networks. https://www.casseroleclub.com/
Category Management	Is a critical aspect of procurement and supply chain management and enables an organisation to establish a full understanding of the potential value to be derived from category areas, commodities and/or markets supporting decision making on categories, consolidation of spend into appropriate category areas, availability of commodities within those category areas and associated market risks involved in their acquisition.
CIPS	Chartered Institute of Purchasing and Supply, as a professional body for the procurement and supply profession, is using its global standard, network, education, expertise and charter for public good to ensure that procurement and supply chain management professionals have the capabilities and responsibility to deliver sustainability goals for their organisations. Other professional bodies are available.
Companies House	Incorporates and dissolves limited companies. Register of company information. Companies House is an executive agency, sponsored by the Department for Business, Energy & Industrial Strategy.
Contango	No, not a kind of South American dance, but a supplement paid by a purchaser for the supplier to retain goods bought as futures until they are delivered. Not in this book but handy to fling around at meetings and at the pub quiz.
Contract Management	should be used as a mechanism to manage relationships and/or assets; to optimise life cycle costs; and to enable and track sustainable outcomes and commitments.
CPO	Chief Procurement Officer.
CSR	Corporate Social Responsibility.
Dun & Bradstreet	Used for Risk Management Solutions to manage credit exposure, D&B Sales & Marketing Solutions to find profitable customers and D&B Supply Management Solutions to manage suppliers efficiently. www.dnb.com
Early Supplier Involvement (ESI)	ESI is a concept that has been around in the commercial word for many years and is, most often, aligned to performance, rather than conformance specifications. It can provide insight to market-leading innovative technologies and solutions which could assist the commercial professional to think creatively.

Tool, technique, process or model	Brief Description
Equifax	Business info services and latest news, to obtaining a copy of your credit file or accessing other services. www.equifax.co.uk
Experian	Experian is an information services provider. Their Business Express service helps organisations determine the credit worthiness of suppliers, using a Commercial Delphi scorecard and many other publicly and privately available data sources. https://www.businessexpress-uk.com/
'Four Box' Supplier Preferencing Analysis	Analysis tool to understand how your supplier views you as a buyer.
GoodSAM	An alternative to Traditional Top Down Public Service Delivery involving augmenting capacity of public services with volunteers. https://www.goodsamapp.org/
Kraljic Model	Peter Kraljic created the Portfolio Purchasing Model (1983), which is a model/tool that compares supply risk and criticality against potential profit impact. He is also the author of *Purchasing must become Supply*.
Market and Supply Chain Analysis	Looks at how market structures are the source of significant competition, innovation and the ability to achieve value for money for stakeholders. An in-depth understanding of them through analysis is critical to determining the procurement strategy and the way in which to achieve best value. It is the role of procurement professionals to continuously explore, research and assess and future proof opportunities to achieve competitive value for taxpayers' money.
MoSCoW Analysis	MoSCoW Analysis to determine, for each activity, whether it Must, Could, Should or Won't be included in your specification.
Nemo dat quod non habet	A Latin phrase like this one is a fantastic device for adding weight and gravitas to what is, essentially, a simple action. Try making them up and impressing people. No one will ever challenge you for fear of appearing dumb. This one means: No one can give what he does not have. Also, not in the book but worth knowing anyway!
One Source – D&B	The OneSource® Business Browser SM family of business information subscriptions provides robust, integrated information on public and private companies, industries and executives worldwide. www.onesource.com
Open Voice Factory	An alternative to Traditional Top Down Public Service Delivery involving (digital) social innovation. https://equalitytime.github.io/TheOpenVoiceFactory-site/
OPEX	Operational Expenditure.
OSR	Operational Statement of Requirement.
Outcome	The effects and results that the business or its customers wants or needs to achieve. The noun outcome refers to the result of a process, but recently, when joined with the word 'based', it has become jargon within a variety of industries, and you'll see uses like outcome-based medicine and outcome-based budgeting.

Tool, technique, process or model	Brief Description
Output	The actions, activities or process that contribute to achieving an outcome.
PESTLE Analysis	An analysis to understand the environment considering political, economic, social, technology, legal and environmental factors. Normally used to observe the external environment but focused on the environment within your organisation in Chapter 1 – 'Know yourself and your organisation'.
Plimsoll Analysis	Provides intelligence and analysis of suppliers and the market that they operate in.
Porter's 5 Forces	A framework for analysing an organisation's competitive environment used to shape procurement strategy.
Reuters	Reuters, through its Multex services, provides global broker and independent research, business information worldwide plus events calendar, SEC filings, market data and other third-party information.
ROAD©	Framework for approaching pre-procurement in complex procurements.
SMART metrics	Specific, Measurable, Assignable, Realistic and Timely metrics.
Social Value	https://www.local.gov.uk/social-value-statement
Spend Analysis	Allows an in-depth understanding of the way in which money is spent and whether return on investment and best value are being achieved within the organisation. It helps procurement to drive cost, value and efficiency benefits out of the supply chain by highlighting opportunities for collaboration, cost reduction, price standardisation, consolidation, rationalisation, compliance management, performance management or other targeted procurement-related initiatives.
Stakeholder Map	The result of a stakeholder mapping exercise, during which the key stakeholders for the procurement are identified, grouped, and plotted on a diagram
STEEPLED Analysis	A strategic planning tool that can be used across all business functions to discover, evaluate, organise and track external risk … It can also reveal a change in direction within your business environment that can help you shape your response to the change rather than be caught out by it.
Supply Chain Management	Focuses on the continuous planning, developing, controlling, informing and monitoring of actions within and between supply chain links so that an integrated supply process meets organisational strategic goals. From a policy perspective, the deeper the supplier chain the more opportunity there is to support investment and development in policy objectives to support fair and ethical trade, equality on workforce matters, and access for SMEs and the third sector in sub-contract organisations.
Supply Positioning tool	Sometimes called the Kraljic model or Segmentation Tool.
Supply Preference Model (SPM)	Developed by Steele and Court in 1996, and it allows a commercial professional to understand how suppliers view them and their requirements and is the converse of Kraljic.

Tool, technique, process or model	Brief Description
Supplier Relationship Management	Presents opportunities to better understand and optimise a supplier's capability and capacity and consider how to improve processes or utilise overall resource more effectively to deliver greater value. It also allows for a more informed assessment and management of risk to the procurement organisation.
Sustainable procurement tools	https://www.procurementjourney.scot/route-3/develop-strategy/profiling-commodityservice/sustainable-procurement
TfL Unified API	An alternative to Traditional Top Down Public Service Delivery involving open data innovation. https://tfl.gov.uk/info-for/open-data-users/unified-api
TrustonTap	An alternative to Traditional Top Down Public Service Delivery involving Government acting as a 'matchmaker'. https://www.trustontap.com/
Whole life costing (WLC)	WLC considers all the costs associated when making a purchase from pre-acquisition through to end of life and is commonly referred to as 'cradle to grave'. It also considers costs that are sometimes overlooked, including environmental and the social impact factors.

Index

Page numbers in *italic* refer to Figures and Tables

Endorsements

'Ian McPherson and his team of commercial and procurement experts will walk your team to commercial excellence. Leaders, contract managers and procurement professionals in the public sector need this book.'

Simon Terry, CEO, 4C Associates

'For those who care about supply chain this book is a godsend. It is not about systems, process, structures and reporting lines. If you want such advice, try an internet search for the answers. This book is different. It is different because it is about real life and written by practitioners, probably people much like you.'

Paul Alexander, Teaching Fellow, University of Portsmouth

'At a time where the procurement profession is increasingly in the public eye, Ian McPherson's publication brings into sharp focus the vital role that procurement professionals play in both the public and private sectors. Ian's book challenges the previous, sometimes held assumption, that procurement is all about getting the best possible price and being hardwired into year-on-year savings, which of course are important and an operational essential. Increasingly, however, the long-term strategic skill imperatives, not to mention corporate social responsibility (CSR), value-based procurement (VBP) and the circular economy, will be key tools needed in the procurement professional's arsenal. As Ian suggests in this excellent book, we can only achieve real success by working together with all internal and external partners and by understanding the commercial and economic, as well as the sustainable, strategic imperatives.'

James 'Jim' Spittle FCILT, Chairman of the NHS Supply Chain (Supply Chain Coordination Limited)

'A masterful mini-opus--a cornucopia of insightful, engaging, witty, and invaluable 'news-you-can-use' on the use of legal counsel. And, while I understand the book in its entirety focuses on supply chain management, the (legal) chapter's honest, direct and jargon-free advice is surely applicable beyond the realm of supply chain management–in fact, to the individual lay person, in general. The section 'If you can't beat 'em, join 'em' is brilliant – cogent, creative, wise counsel for all companies.'

Jerry Haar, Professor in the Department of International Business at Florida International University

'I wish a book of this kind and calibre had been around when I started my first card business in the 1980s. Though I took my eye off the ball while pursuing my professional golf career, I could have done with this support – a business caddie, if you like – to help me navigate the business world at the same time. It's a master class in planning and execution.'

Garry Logan, PGA professional golfer and founder of Paperbox--Xmas Box.

'I am not a procurement specialist. But, as an operational logistician, I appreciate the vital importance of effective supply and support chains created and managed by professionals who know how to do their job. And any of those professionals would benefit from the experiences, commentary and insights offered in this book. Very far from being a 'how to' manual – thankfully – instead it provides a compelling, environment-wide narrative that will add holistically to the knowledge of even the most capable practitioner. Beyond that, for those who lead and employ these practitioners, this book should give them the confidence to trust and empower them to deploy their skills and experience to deliver value through risk-balanced and innovative solutions to enduring problems.'

Richard Hill CBE, Air Vice Marshal, Director Support Transformation Ministry of Defence, Chief Logistician (Royal Air Force)

'I have worked in the public and charity sector all my professional career surrounded by people who are passionate about what they do and the causes that they serve. They want to do the right thing but so often achieving that can be fraught with endless regulations, processes and procedures and perceived bureaucracy. This can be so all-consuming to navigate that they are side tracked, or worse, fail to engage at all. This can undermine and put at risk the very thing they are trying so desperately to support and enable to succeed – their business. This book brings clarity to the entire procurement process and provides a useful insight on how to get the balance and focus right, to build solid foundations in all areas of practice and enable the public sector to be more focused and commercial in its outlook. This is long-awaited and should form part of every procurement professional's toolkit and all staff who want to make a difference in this field.'

Alison Jarvis, Director of Financial Operations, Cardiff University

'Anyone who has set out to buy goods knows that can be the start of a tortuous journey – no more so than in the construction sector. It often evokes more questions than answers but, thankfully, lots of these are answered in this very accessible little guidebook to the commercial world.'

Jorge Peralta Urquiza, Architect, CallisonRTKL

'I have been working in supply chain management for well over 35 years and sometimes there is a contribution to the profession that you just know is really going to make a difference, I believe Ian's book is one of those. I really enjoyed the collaborative style that comes through in every chapter, the examples that bring the points alive and the 'how to' pointers that allows the reader to relate to other practitioners in the 'decision'. The procurement profession has seen a substantive rise in the use of shared outcome purchasing and this book shows why. Having started in procurement and ending up in sales, I can sense where Ian and his collaborators are coming from, an ethical profession, trying to drive ever-increasing value in a fast moving world and finding a way to share best practice between public and private sectors along the way. This book will be valuable to all involved in buying (and selling) both products and services and I congratulate Ian for having the foresight to pull it all together.'

Paul Brooks FCILT FIOD, Director, Go Further Consulting

'This book provides a much-needed practitioner perspective on the challenge of procurement. By reflecting on over 30 years of experience in both public and private sector, the author's personal account describes the tools, approaches and lessons gained over this diverse career. It demonstrates how known techniques and frameworks support the strategic and operational decisions made but also, and importantly, the personal 'soft' skills and approaches required to create success. The content is an excellent 'check list' for any procurement professional to reflect on, enabling those readers to avoid pit falls and traps and also gain competitive advantage by working with suppliers more effectively'

Professor Richard Wilding OBE, Full Professor & Chair of Supply Chain Strategy, Cranfield School Of Management

This is a timely publication; indeed it must be said that such a publication is long overdue! The title alone must herald the ethos that professionals in public sector procurement and supply chain management environments must adopt in order to enable more effective performance for their respective organisations.

For too long there has been an approach in the public sector environment that is based upon not being open to criticism, with a need to ensure that rules and regulations must be adhered to at all costs – which leads to an ethos of caution with an assumption that one must prove that that they are not guilty of any supplier preference (and therefore suboptimal solutions). Such an ethos frequently suppresses professional judgement, which can be overcome by the sound and successful approaches that are presented in this book. It recognises the challenges of procurement and supply chain management in such public sector contexts, yet provides proven approaches that can vastly improve organisational performance – and enhance the satisfaction of those professionals involved and thus encourage further professional development.

The contents enable belief, confidence and indeed courage, to be employed in contextual decision making through a straightforward, structured and enjoyable set of integrated relevant proven techniques and approaches.

This is a valuable asset for all public sector procurement and supply chain management professionals, which I thoroughly commend.

Dr David M Moore, Director, Centre for Defence Acquisition Cranfield University, Defence Academy